The Slave Across the Street

The Slave Across the Street

Theresa Flores

arrow books

Published by Arrow Books 2013

2 4 6 8 10 9 7 5 3 1

First published in Great Britain in 2013 by
Arrow Books
Random House, 20 Vauxhall Bridge Road,
London SW1V 2SA

www.randomhouse.co.uk

Addresses for companies within The Random House Group Limited can be
found at: www.randomhouse.co.uk/offices.htm

The Random House Group Limited Reg. No. 954009

A CIP catalogue record for this book is available from the British Library.

ISBN 9780099588139

The Random House Group Limited supports the Forest Stewardship
Council® (FSC®), the leading international forest-certification organisation.
Our books carrying the FSC label are printed on FSC®-certified paper. FSC
is the only forest-certification scheme supported by the leading environmental
organisations, including Greenpeace. Our paper procurement policy can be
found at: www.randomhouse.co.uk/environment

Printed and bound by CPI Group (UK) Ltd, Croydon, CR0 4YY

To my beautiful children: Samantha,
Helena and Trey.
To Lee for being my rock.
To God for blessing me with His Grace and
giving me strength.
And to all those who don't have a voice.

Contents

Acknowledgments

First and foremost I want to honor my family; my three beautiful children for being by my side while I wrote this book. I thank them for putting up with my tirades, my emotional breakdowns and my frustrations while I processed and healed by putting down my life on paper. Without them I wouldn't have had the courage or strength to endure the re-occurring nightmares. They saw how hard this was on their mum but always supported my decision to embark on this journey, even when they were afraid when I quit my career as a social worker with a regular paycheck to speak out full-time. They had the difficult task of explaining to their friends about my past and had to defend me sometimes too. At times they were ridiculed for what happened to me but they continued to support me every step of the way.

My oldest daughter, Samantha, with her tender heart couldn't bear the thought of something like this happening to her mum and wrote her college entrance essay on how proud she was of me. Helena, my strong-willed second daughter, took the issue of sex trafficking very seriously. She volunteered for organizations fighting it, has written papers on it for school and had heavy debates with people who 'just don't get it'. And my dear son Trey, the youngest, cried after he heard me tell my story on the radio when I didn't know he was listening. Trey asked me, 'How could a man treat a woman this way?' And I knew at that moment he would treat women equally and I wished we had more men in the world like him. All three have volunteered to help me with my mission to fight trafficking and had to endure their home looking like a war zone with the posters, papers and items on the issue of modern slavery. Their love gave me hope to get through each day and see a better one the next. They gave me back my smile, my laughter and a song.

My three younger brothers have stood by my side at movie screenings watching their sister sharing the secret she had held in for so long. They cried with me, stood up for me and explained to doubters how this had happened to me and with no one knowing.

And to Lee, my fiancé, for helping me learn to trust again. For wiping my tears away, holding me during my nightmares, making me smile and laugh again and for bringing balance to my life. Lee never doubted me and has supported me with every decision I have made, even when I went back to where it all happened to do presentations on trafficking. Thanks for talking me through the hard times, making me realize that when things got tough I had a purpose to keep on living. Plus someday, I will beat you at canasta!

Thanks to Mike Bucy, the first person who allowed me to tell my full story. He listened, held me and offered suggestions on what to do. Although it took years to find another accepting person to hear me, he paved the way for my healing on several different levels. It is only natural that he is employed in one of the caring professions.

I would like to thank my friends and co-workers who supported me while I tackled this seemingly insurmountable mountain. After years of feeling as if I carried the weight of the world on my shoulders I found precious friends who didn't blink an eye when I told them my story.

My friend Natalie, who was the first to hold my nightmare in her hands, proofread it and still felt proud to know me. Her friendship empowered me to continue on my journey until I had completed it. And to Bev, who has ministered to me, cried with me, laughed, taught me about the Bible and helped me process my emotions and pain. She provided foresight to see the length of my path, giving me strength to travel along the hard part.

Thanks to God for allowing me to stand here today, alive, healthy, no longer broken and finally able to tell my story. My emotional journey while writing would not have been possible had it not been for the support from so many people who have touched my life. People who prayed for me, provided a circle of protection while I shared my story publicly and comforted me when I felt overwhelmed.

Lastly, thanks to Jason Chatraw at Ampelon Publishing for believing in the importance of this issue and taking a chance to publish on it. To Julia Twaites at Random House for seeing the value in sharing my story. And to Andrea Picco for her passion and creative eye and using it to create a student documentary about my experiences. To Sandy Shepard and Given Kachepa, Clarkston Community Church, especially Pastor Bonnie, NAAG, Michigan State Troopers, The Salvation Army, the Central Ohio Coalition to Rescue and Restore, the Collaborative Initiative Against Human Trafficking in Cleveland, Ohio. To all the wonderful Catholic nuns – Mercy, Dominican of Peace (Sr. Nadine), Humility of Mary (Karen, Toby & Ann), Providence Franciscan, and Notre Dame to name a few – for their support and eagerness to combat this injustice head on. They listened, never judged or doubted and gave me unconditional love and acceptance. Thanks to the Soroptimist International for their mission to help women and girls have a better life and awarding me for my work. Thanks to the Doma International, Polaris Project, the National Underground Railroad Freedom Center in Cincinnati, Love 146, WAR, Shared Hope and to all the people in Ohio who helped me find my voice, who gave me the determination to finish this book and share my pain to educate others on modern day-slavery.

Preface

When I was a child, my mother would tuck me into bed every night and read me a book about Catholic saints. My favorite story was about my patron saint, Teresa, the Little Flower. The story said that on the day Teresa died, the sky opened and rained roses. A picture showed Saint Teresa bending over the bed of a child who slept sweetly like a little cherub. The smiling Saint Teresa had laid a single rose in the open hand of the sleeping child. I dreamed of being worthy enough to have Saint Teresa visit me during my sleep and bless me with one of her divine flowers. I would lie in bed with my hand open and try to sleep without moving it all night. Each morning when I awoke, I would look to see if there was a rose. Of course there never was and I would think, if I am better today, more special and worthy, then I will be granted a rose.

In 1988 when I was twenty-three years old, I watched a movie that made me wonder about the intervention of the divine in my own life. In *The Seventh Sign*, Demi Moore plays a woman who is torn between her everyday struggles and her religion. She has a recurring dream in which she is confronted by an evil man in ancient garb, carrying a clay pot. He throws one of the woman's friends, a kind-faced young man (who is Jesus), violently to the ground. Repeatedly the evil man demands of Demi Moore, 'Do you know this man?' If she publicly admits her friendship with Jesus, acknowledging she is a Christian, she faces a tortuous death by the Romans. If she denies the truth, takes the easy way out, she will be turning away from His rich and unconditional friendship. By denying her faith, she will lose her soul.

Since I was a young girl, I have had this same dream. It feels like a nightmare, really. I ask myself what I would do in a similar position but the dream never answers that question. Why was I so torn making this decision? I was confident deep in my soul that I would freely give my life for a stranger if I had to. If I was confronted in a dark alley, a corner store, or parking garage, I would have no fear of facing death if it meant jumping in front of a bullet for a stranger.

What does this dream have to do with slavery? While I was enslaved as a teenager I faced similarly important and life-threatening decisions each day. I had to ask myself whether or not to deny or tarnish my family's name. Which was the worse of two evils? I was devoted to my faith, my future husband and my church's requirement to retain my virginity. I felt that I didn't have any choice in what path I followed.

When Saint Agnes was thirteen, still a child, she was faced with a similar dilemma. Yet she never floundered in her faith. She refused to marry a man who offered her jewels and riches as she had promised herself to God. Forced to decide, she chose her faith. As a result she was condemned to death but there was a law against executing a virgin. So the man who had proposed to her had her dragged through the streets naked and put into a brothel. Later she was released, held trial and put to death. She spent her short life in sexual slavery for this one decision.

I chose my family. As a result, I also endured sexual slavery. Despite the horror, I never wavered in my decision. Although others may not comprehend this, God understood. He helped me face the bonds and torture. Later He blessed me with the ability to tell this story. My experience shows that bad things can happen to anyone. We choose our paths from the options we have available to us at that moment. And whether our choice is right or wrong, the Lord helps us cope with the results of that decision.

I prayed for the pain to go away, to make it stop and for a way out of my nightmare. And when the trauma was finally over, He helped me put back the pieces of my soul. When I was healthy enough, He helped me find a purpose for it.

It took years for me to realize that I do have choices. I can say no. But I was powerless during those years. Later on, when I was released from captivity, I turned that power around and used sex to my advantage. But that extreme left me unhappy, empty and hollow like a shell. Even on my own terms, it didn't satisfy me. It took me years to realize that the physical union between two people is sacred. It is the divine knitting together of the physical and the spiritual. Both individuals surrender their power each other and then they are blessed with a truly spiritual experience in the merging of two into one.

My abuse lasted two long years, a small fraction of time in relation to the age I am now. What followed was over twenty years of silence and keeping my secret at all costs. It is the nightmares that can last an eternity. Years passed between my abuse and being brave enough to write each chapter of this book I repeatedly cracked open Pandora's Box, only to slam it shut again each time. I was afraid to pry it open, afraid to expose my deepest and darkest secrets one at a time. I finally gained the spiritual strength I needed to peek in once more and confront my inner demons head on, this time for the sake of healing others.

I completed the book as part of my healing. My abuse happened nearly thirty-one years ago but the trauma no longer holds me captive. The growing question as I wrote the book was not the title, but what to name my traumatic experience. As humans, we require a one- or two-word label that sums up everything we need to know about one's personality, their medical or mental condition, race and ethnicity, religion, education, and political views. I struggled to find a label for what I had experienced. I felt that I couldn't accurately finish the book without it. I needed to know the term for myself.

Then, in June of 2006, a co-worker, who is a deeply spiritual woman, came to me and handed me a flyer on a conference.

'Theresa, I need you to do me a favor. I signed up to attend this conference and I have a schedule conflict. I need you to go for me please and besides I get the feeling that you need to be there.' I glanced at the flyer. It was for a Human Trafficking Conference.

Hmm. I didn't know much about the issue but I was a bilingual social worker and thought that since so many of my clients were international immigrants and it was already paid for, I might as well go.

'OK,' I told her, still puzzled as to why she thought I needed to go. We had had long talks but I had never revealed my past to her.

I circled the date of the conference on my calendar and must have received four phone calls from people asking me for appointments on that day but instead of changing my plans I decided to help my co-worker out and arrange these appointments for another time. I'm so glad I did.

The night before the conference I told my kids, 'Mummy has an important conference to go to tomorrow so I need all of you to go to school tomorrow and be good,' still not realizing why I needed to be there so badly.

The next morning, as I sat in the audience of the packed auditorium, I learned that the definition of Human Trafficking, from the U.S. Department of State, is essentially when *'A person is being blackmailed, coerced, threatened to do something they don't want to do for commercial sex or labor.'*

The words rang in my head as they were discussed on the stage.

Tears started to flow down my cheeks as a fog seemed to lift from my being. I wasn't the only one? There were others? How could that be? How did I not know this before?

Members of the audience asked many questions: 'How many people does this happen to? Are there laws against it? Why don't the victims come forward?'

There were no answers that satisfied the confused and curious audience, who were mostly professionals and were stunned by what they were learning, especially when the speaker told them, 'No. We don't have many laws against it. We don't know how many victims there are. Very few victims come forward and prosecute.'

The audience was told that it usually happens to children involved in the foster care system, those from broken homes or runaways or the impoverished, minorities or immigrants. But I had come from a loving, financially secure family. Sure, we had our own dysfunctions, like most families, but I had professional parents, caring siblings and a privileged lifestyle. I didn't look like the typical person this sort of thing happened to. I didn't fit the mold.

I sat quietly in my seat, listening to the shocked conference participants asking for more explanations. It was then that I decided it was time; time to tell the world about what happens in America. That this happened to me.

Dazed, I realized after all these years that I had found my word. It had taken from the time I was fifteen years old until I was forty-one to meet understanding strangers with kind eyes, and receive a warm hug from another survivor with an offer to help me. I had found my label. Found my truth. It was the beginning of the process of coming to terms with the reality that I'd been a white, middle-class teenager, a budding track star, an all-American, Catholic girl, and yet I was a victim of human trafficking.

I had been commercially, sexually exploited as a child. I had been a teenage sex slave.

1

Escape

The bell rang, announcing the end of the day. It was Friday. A smile spread across my face. I couldn't remember the last time I had smiled during school. My steps were lighter as I made my way through the crowded hallway towards my locker. As usual, Daniel was standing there. He had a dark air to him and even after all I had gone through, all he had done to me, I still found it very sexy. The fear I felt made my stomach hurt, yet at the same time my heart yearned for his love. My body felt so confused, though this wasn't anything new for me.

I didn't look at him directly and tried to concentrate on opening the combination lock. 21–9–3 click. 'Theresa, *habibi*,' he said, using the Arabic word for sweetheart, 'do you want to go for a ride? My brother is pressuring me. We need to figure out what to do. He wants an answer.'

The question wasn't really a question. I knew it was a demand as usual. I wouldn't let him get me down. I had waited for this day for what seemed like a lifetime. 'No thank you,' I said politely yet timidly.

I had uttered the word 'no' only once before to Daniel. But he had ignored it that day two years ago, which had led to the utter mess I was in now. Since then, the word 'no' had never crossed my lips, not until today. He just stood there stunned. At that moment he looked tired. This had been going on for a long time for both of us.

'What did you say? Theresa, we need to talk!'

He started muttering under his breath in Arabic. I tried to act like I didn't understand him. I took my folders and purse out of my locker and shut the door. Since it was my last day of school, I had already turned my books in to the office earlier that day. 'Daniel, I am going home. Goodbye.'

I was shaking inside. He had never made a scene in school before. Would he do it now, when I had so much on the line? Would he force me to go with him? Would he hit the locker and yell at me? I turned and walked away as fast as I could. I knew I couldn't turn around and look into his eyes and do what I needed to do.

As I walked toward the exit, I could hear everyone around me making plans for the weekend. But I kept my head down, moving quickly past them, and when I opened and walked through the side door of the school I vowed never to walk back through that door ever again.

I ran home, passing my younger brother Patrick on the way.

'Hey T.T.,' Patrick yelled. T.T. was his nickname for me, or sometimes just T, which other people had also started to call me. 'I need to tell you something,' he yelled after me.

But I kept on going as fast as I could. I didn't want anything to dampen this feeling. I felt elated, like I was jumping from cloud to cloud with each step.

I suddenly heard car tires screech nearby and froze dead in my tracks. I dared to turn around and look. It was just some kids from school fooling around. I breathed out a huge sigh of relief, but quickly became serious again. It was too early to celebrate. That sound of a car had reminded me that this wasn't over. I wasn't free yet.

There were still plenty of things that could happen before tomorrow morning that could turn out badly. Behind me, I kept hearing my little brother yelling, 'T, wait for me.' But I kept running.

I slowly turned the handle on the front door and

walked into organized chaos. There was activity everywhere. People with tan shorts and navy blue polo shirts with the logo 'Mayflower Moving' on the upper corner were all over the place. I made my way to the kitchen and saw my mum bent over a large brown removals box, gently placing her prize possessions inside, praying out loud for nothing to break. Several other staff had been assigned to the kitchen to help her pack. My parents entertained regularly, mostly for my dad's work, so Mum had many pieces of fine china dishes and sparkling crystal glasses and bowls. The kitchen, the heart of our home, was the biggest job in the house.

'Be very careful with that! I don't want anything broken,' she barked at one of the removal company packers. She must have sensed me because she didn't even look up as she said, 'Theresa, go upstairs and pack your suitcase. You need a pair of pajamas and one change of clothes. That's it. There isn't room for any other stuff.'

No 'Hi honey. How was your day?' I felt a bit put out but I guess she was concentrating on the very large job of moving a family of six halfway across the country at a moment's notice. It's not like this was the first time for us. We moved every two years and by the time I was eighteen years old, I had attended three high schools in four years, lived in four states, and moved ten times in my life. We all hated moving as it disrupted our lives so much, and this time Mum didn't seem happy about it either. My parents had been fighting a lot lately. Mum was tired of moving and had become really involved in this area. She was in the Gourmet Supper Club where couples got together monthly to research foods from all around the world and then assigned one another a different dish and drink to make. She also loved acting in the local theater and had a part-time job working to assign placements for international students. Now she was being uprooted and had to move far from her life here and her friends. We all were.

But this time I was beyond excited. I wasn't upset that I hadn't said goodbye to all my friends. I was so close to tasting freedom I could smell it. I ran up the stairs to my room at the end of the hall and stopped suddenly. There were two strange men in my room whispering, taping the mirror on my large dresser. They turned when they saw me come in, smiled and said, 'Hello there young lady. Is there anything we can *help* you with?'

I instantly felt uncomfortable; this flirtation was the last thing I wanted to deal with now. 'No, sorry, I need to get my things. Could you pack another room for now?' I asked.

When they had left I closed my bedroom door

and sat down on my bed with my suitcase, pondering what to take with me. I started packing the few clothes I was taking away. I opened the drawer to my nightstand and took out my diary that was carefully hidden underneath a stack of books. My diary was sacred to me. It was the only place where I could release all my feelings, thoughts and nightmares. I wrote in it religiously every day. It was my best friend, the only confidant I had. I poured out my soul in those pages, along with a good amount of tears. I placed it in the suitcase and then went to my closet and found the hiding place for all my letters to Jimmy, my long-distance boyfriend. I carefully placed the packet of letters next to my diary, threw in a few novels and then zipped up the suitcase.

I looked around the room slowly and reflected on the few nice memories I had of there. I remembered singing to albums on my record player with my little brothers, recording them playing their musical instruments, rather badly, for our grandparents who lived far away. I looked over to my dresser and sitting there in perfect order was my most prize possession, my perfume bottle collection. It comprised over thirty bottles of various colors, sizes and shapes. Some were shaped like fruit; some were glass balls and one special bottle turned into a rose with a long stem when you turned it upside down. Many of the bottles were tiny and fit in the palm of my hand. The smell didn't matter to me, in fact most were empty, but they were special because each one was given to me by my grandmothers. I was their oldest grandchild and every time I looked at their old bottles that they had passed down to me, I felt their unconditional love. I carefully placed these bottles in newspaper and added them to my suitcase.

Deep in concentration, I jumped from the shrill of the phone in my room ringing. Oh no! Please not now, I thought. I couldn't. I just couldn't. I was so close to escaping. I slowly picked up the phone. 'Hello?' I answered softly.

'I can't believe it. How could you do this to us? We thought you were our friend!' Paula, a girl from school, was crying dramatically on the other end of the line. What a relief.

'I'm so sorry, Paula. I just found out! It was really sudden, I know. I just hate leaving here and all my friends!' I lied.

Paula was the first girl I had met when I moved here two and a half years earlier. We weren't particularly close but she was always nice to me. 'I just have to see you and say goodbye! You can't just leave without a goodbye. What is your new address? We have to write every week!' she exclaimed.

I had to think quickly. How had she found out I was leaving? What would I say? We were good friends but no one could find out where I was going until I was far away.

'Yes, we will write every week but the problem is I don't know what my new address is yet. The house isn't ready and we are staying somewhere temporarily. How about if you just give me your address and I will write to you first?' I lied again. Well, *part* of it was true.

'OK, but we have to say goodbye in person. Come over and I will give you my address. I'll have Janie come over too. We will both miss you so much.'

There simply wasn't any way out of it. I agreed and told her I would be over shortly. I rushed out of my room and ran right into Patrick. 'Hey, why didn't you wait for me?' he said breathlessly. 'Mum told you that you need to walk with me. I was trying to tell you something.'

I put all the pieces of the puzzle together.

'It was you! You told Paula we were moving. How many times have I told you not to talk to my friends? Did you tell them where we were moving? Please say you didn't!' I yelled at him. I just couldn't believe it. His stupid mistake could cost me my life. I was so mad.

'T, I didn't tell them where. I thought you did. Why didn't you tell them? Aren't they your friends?' He seemed confused.

'Stay out of my business, Pat. You don't know anything,' I shouted.

'I'm sorry. I didn't mean it. I didn't know,' he said sincerely. He seemed very upset.

'I know you didn't. It's OK.' I felt bad and softened a little, it wasn't his fault. I was just so nervous with worry.

I walked back into the kitchen. My mum was in the same spot as when I had gone upstairs. She was writing on the boxes in a big, black permanent marker. This time she looked up. She seemed so tired. 'Mum, I need to go to Paula's house and say goodbye to her and Janie. Please. Just for a minute. I won't be long.'

'Didn't you say goodbye at school? Theresa, I need you to help Mike and David get packed. They are sick and I don't have time to do it.'

'I know. I will help them as soon as I get back, I promise. It will only take me a minute. I will be right back,' I pleaded.

She thought about it and reluctantly agreed. 'But you have to ride your bike. We already shipped your car,' she said as she resumed her work.

Oh no. Ride a bike? I gave up riding my bike after all of this started because of the pain it caused me. But this was the only way. I ran through the laundry room into the garage and saw my two little brothers

Mike and David coming up the driveway from school. They had just been diagnosed with walking pneumonia and looked pretty sick but still seemed to have an amazing amount of energy. 'Hey, T. You going for a bike ride? Can we come too? Please?' they begged.

'No, boys. I need to be somewhere. I will be right back and then I will help you pack. OK?'

'We don't want to pack. We want to go to the park.'

'I know, but you need to pack all your stuffed animals and Lego so the removal man don't lose them. Then when I get back, we will play hide and seek around the tower of boxes. OK?'

'OK,' they said in unison and turned to go inside the house.

I gingerly got on the bike and began to ride, trying not to put my full weight on the seat. I cringed with each bump I hit. I took the back way and prayed my brothers weren't watching me. I crossed over the main road and into Paula's estate. We all said our goodbyes and I promised to write to them first. Another lie, as I had no intention of ever contacting anyone from here again.

When I got home Dad was around for dinner. He had been living temporarily in Connecticut for the new job at his work's headquarters and was commuting back and forth on the weekends. He was home for a little while to help with the move. We had a treat in the form of pizza and fizzy drinks. There was a little bit of tension in the room and I put it down to Mum being tired from supervising the removal men all day and not being happy with having to leave. 'Hey, Dad, do the phones still work?' asked Patrick.

'Yes. We have to keep them on until tomorrow in case the removal company calls. They won't officially be turned off until Monday. But we will be in Connecticut by then,' he replied.

I felt the color drain from my face. Oh no. There was still a chance I wouldn't make it. They could still call me. And if they found out about the move, there was no way they were going to let me go without a fight. A fight *they* would win.

We all went to bed early because we needed to get up and on the road as soon as the removal men arrived in the morning. They would load up the furniture and boxes in the huge Mayflower Moving vans while we drove halfway across the country.

That night, I tossed and turned in bed, fearful that the phone next to my bed would ring. I didn't risk turning if off or unplugging it. There was one time when I hadn't answered the phone and I vividly recalled the physical punishment I had endured at the trafficker's hands the next night. Around midnight, the usual time the call would come, I started pacing back and forth in my room. Around

2 a.m. I couldn't stand it any longer; I started to break down in fear. The tears flowed down my cheeks. It was all too much for any person to handle, let alone a seventeen-year-old girl. I was hours away from escaping but I knew there were no guarantees that this would happen.

I decided to take my last bath in this house to calm down. I went to the bathroom and ran the bath with steaming hot water. As the tub filled up, I found a towel and a bar of soap to help clean away the past. As I soaked, I listened for the phone. I prayed silently that I would be able to move away in silence and my escape would finally set me free.

When I climbed out of the tub, I gingerly blotted my sensitive skin dry. It was still bruised and tender from the last time I had been forced to service strange men. I put my pajamas back on and climbed into bed. The clock read 3 a.m. Phew. The coast was clear. They had never called this late before. I fell fast asleep instantly, exhausted from the worry, but it was not a peaceful sleep. I dreamed that my trafficker snatched me from my bed in the middle of the night and my family drove off without me in the morning heading to our new home, the car loaded up, without realizing I wasn't with them.

At the break of dawn I heard my father's voice booming down the hall to wake us all up. 'Time to go!'

Dad was very excited about this new job and

the move. He had told us that he had found the perfect home for his family. It was a large colonial-style house with four bedrooms, a huge yard out front and swimming pool in the backyard. We were close to the beach and only an hour from New York City. The only problem was that we couldn't move in straight away as Dad had gotten a good deal on the house because the current owners were divorcing. The divorce was messy and it would be several months until the courts finalized everything. But my dad had been commuting back and forth while we finished up the school semester and he was anxious to get his family all moved to the same place so he had rented a summer vacation home in Milford, one street from the beach. I am certain he hoped we would have a chance to have some quality family time, that he and my mum would restore their marriage that was falling apart and that my mum would meet some nice friends again.

'Let's go, kids, everyone in the van. Bring your suitcases,' he yelled out.

As the van pulled away, I slowly slid to its floor. I tried to peek out the windows to see if there were any cars parked on our street, watching us drive. I still wasn't free. Daniel might have been suspicious yesterday when I said no to him, and could have sent someone over to investigate.

As we drove down the road and went through downtown Detroit I tried not to think about 'that night'. The night I had been kidnapped and left for dead in the inner city. I was so nervous I was nauseous. I lay on the floor of the van as we crossed over the Michigan state line and entered Ohio. When we got on the toll road, I felt my body finally relax. I took a deep breath and fell fast asleep.

'Theresa, you are missing all the scenic sites by sleeping the day away. Wake up!' my mum urged, jolting me awake.

'Burger King. Rickart RVs. Marathon gas ...' My brother Pat read the signs as we passed them. He had a habit of reading signs, trucks, billboards, anything.

I looked around. 'Where are we, Dad?' I asked.

'Pennsylvania. In about an hour we reach New York!' he excitedly answered.

I looked out the back window of the van and watched for about ten minutes. It didn't look like anyone was following us. Was I really free? No more late nights being forced to have sex with strangers? No more threats to kill my family, or people following me and my brothers everywhere? Could this actually be true?

A few hours later as we pulled into a gated community my dad announced, 'Here we are, kids!'

The beach houses were quaint and you could tell

they had been passed down through the generations, each one holding many memories. I could smell the ocean, the salt and the seaweed. My dad drove down a small street and there were bits of sand on the road. He stopped the car.

'Who wants out?' he exclaimed.

'What are you doing? We aren't at the house yet,' my mother objected.

'The kids have been in the car a long time. Let them go roam around and explore while we unload the car at the house.' He gave her a wink. Perhaps he wanted some time alone with her.

We didn't wait for a response – my brothers and I climbed out of the van and dashed for the gate to the beach. We peeled off our shoes, left them in the sand and ran straight to the sea. All four of us dipped our toes into the cold salt water and screeched from the shock of it. While the boys searched for shells and threw seaweed at one another, I walked down the beach. Alone with my thoughts, I pondered the past few years. I found a huge boulder propped perfectly next to the ocean and climbed up on it.

I looked out to the horizon, scanning the ocean, and allowed myself to take the deepest breath possible. I filled up my lungs with the salty tang of air as tears flowed freely down my cheeks. I had made it! I was free. Never could I have imagined that I would be sitting on a beach, a thousand miles away from my traffickers. Free after being held in slavery for two years. I felt truly lucky – lucky to be alive, lucky to have a second chance at life. I vowed at that moment that the old me was dead. I would create a whole new Theresa and no one would ever know about my past or about my sins.

'Hey T. What are you doing sitting on that big rock? Why are you crying? Wanna go get our swim-suits?' Pat asked.

'I got a piece of sand in my eye. That's all. Sure. Let's go check out the new house and get changed.' We gathered our shoes and headed back to our temporary home.

That night I settled down to sleep, a thousand miles away from Daniel and my traffickers. There was no phone in my room. There wasn't even a working phone in the house since it was a rental. It was such a sweet relief. But there also wasn't a bathtub. What would I do without being able to take a bath when I couldn't sleep? Oh well, I told myself, I had the whole ocean one street away. I said my evening prayers and thanked God for giving me my freedom. I closed my eyes, certain that I would sleep better than I had in years. But something happened. This is when the nightmares started.

I could stop the bad thoughts during the daytime,

but at night they came to me in my sleep. I was physically free but mentally I was still held in bondage. Despite my efforts I couldn't stop remembering the horror I had lived through as a teenage sex slave.

2

A ray of sunshine

In those days, it was considered a mixed marriage. Mum was from a large, Catholic family of Irish decent. My father was a White Anglo-Saxon Protestant, commonly known back then as a WASP. Though this caused a small amount of conflict inside the family and at various parishes we belonged to, in general it wasn't a big deal.

My mum was a real beauty. She had blond hair and baby blue eyes and a great figure. She was the life and soul of parties: she loved to entertain, and was very domestically inclined. She was very creative, throwing together centerpieces at the drop of a hat, cooking amazing gourmet meals and making the most of our clothes when my brothers and I were little. She was also a natural-born storyteller and had a gregarious laugh that could be heard throughout the whole house.

Mum ran the entire house and was in charge of us kids when Dad was away, which was a lot. She was a take-charge kind of person, believing that organization and cleanliness were important. When my brothers and I were young, the houses that we lived in weren't comfortable, but a tad on the sterile and cold side.

While Mum was outgoing and extrovert, my father was quiet and introspective. My dad was a kind man of few words. When he spoke you listened, because you knew that whatever he was going to say was important. He loved the outdoors and fixing things, and although he wasn't as outgoing as my mother, he too loved to entertain and show off everything he had worked so hard for. He had high expectations of his children and we didn't want to disappoint him. He wasn't a violent man and when there were disagreements, or one of us had misbehaved, he believed in talking over what we had done rather than raising a hand to us.

My parents hadn't planned on my birth. They had met in college and it was the 1960s. Free love and all that. Mum was only twenty years old and Dad was twenty-two when they met. Dad was studying to be a mechanical engineer and was in his final year of college at a small school in northern Indiana and Mum was going to business school nearby. On Memorial Day weekend at the end of May they had gone with a group of friends to a popular local lake resort to celebrate the holiday and the start of summer. That weekend they talked until late at night, the drinks flowed and they fell in love.

Five months later they were married. My mum had become pregnant and my dad thought it was best if she married him. He felt a sense of responsibility for her so he quit college with only one semester left before graduation. My mother was disappointed about her pregnancy, as she'd had plans to travel the world and not get tied down until she absolutely had to. They ended up moving to my dad's hometown of Akron, Ohio. I was born in March of 1965, the following year. Dad got a good job designing car tires and within nine months had an offer to move to my mum's hometown of Fort Wayne, back in Indiana, with a sales job for General Electric.

In Mum's hometown, she had support from her family while Dad was busy working. Though she had always wanted to travel, and felt slighted that she'd had to move back home, she felt a sense of relief at being in a family setting and having them close by when she needed them most. We were very close to her family. She had one sister and six brothers and the youngest was only ten years older than me. They thought of me as their little sister. They took me sledging, to horse shows, festivals and to ice-cream parlors in search of the best homemade root beer. The boys used me to try to impress girls and even taught me how to drive a stick shift on an old MG auto.

I was born with strawberry-blond hair, a perfect combination of both my mother and father, and had hazel-green eyes. Growing up I was quite girly; I loved anything that was pink with ruffles. I had a canopy bed with multi-colored butterflies covering it and loved to play with my dolls, dress up and pretend to have tea parties. When I was about nine years old my dad built me a playhouse out of wood in the back-yard. It had a front door, windows and I made my brothers play house with me all the time.

As the oldest, I had a tendency to be a bit bossy. I could spend hours playing with my Barbies or playing 'school' with my brothers. I was always the teacher, and in fact I taught my baby brother Michael to read before he started school. My maternal, nurturing spirit that's always been a part of me, was evident in those early years. I enjoyed taking care of my broth-ers, keeping them happy and entertained, and I was very protective of them, making sure that they stayed out of trouble. My parents told me that as I was the oldest this was my responsibility, and I embraced it fully. Because we moved so frequently we only had each other to play with most of the time.

In addition to feminine activities like arts and crafts, I enjoyed playing with the boys, building tire swings and forts in the woods, climbing trees and carving my initials in the wood with a knife as well as racing bikes and fishing. I wasn't scared of anything – except snakes. I loved nature and animals and for a while wanted to be a veterinarian. It was not uncommon for me to bring home wounded birds or orphaned baby rabbits. I had always been taught to stick up for the less fortunate and I believed strongly that everyone was equal and should be treated as such. Later on, as an adolescent, I would get into arguments in class when we discussed race and women's rights issues. I always raised my hand in lessons and was involved in any discussions we had. In my weekly religion class, I even challenged the priest. 'Why can't women be priests?' I asked him, confused by this inequality and wanting to find a sensible answer to it. 'Why can't priests and nuns marry?'

But his answers never satisfied me. When the Catholic Church announced that they would be allowing girls to serve priests during Mass I was the first one to sign up, much to the consternation of the priest who thought I was quite rebellious against their traditions. At the first Mass I served, I made sure

I did a very good job and said to him after, 'See. Girls can do just as good a job as boys!'

So, anyway, I was quite a feisty little thing and for the most part I was a happy kid, smiled a lot, was nicknamed 'Sunshine' and had a very loud, distinctive, gregarious laugh that people teased me about. I must have inherited it from my mother. I was also a very good student and loved to please adults, but I wasn't exactly what my mum called 'street smart'. Common sense seemed to have passed me by as I was very trusting and naive.

As the years passed, after my mum had my three brothers, she seemed to get sadder. I presume it was due to the unexpected change in direction her life had taken. She hadn't planned to end up being in her twenties with four young children and a husband who was away at work all the time in order to support his family and grow his career. Mum loved all of us very much but wasn't a touchy-feely, doting, maternal figure who coddled a child to her bosom. That just wasn't her nature. She was more of a 'hands on' person who took pleasure in teaching us how to cook, enjoy crafts and getting involved in our activities.

As a young child I sucked my thumb excessively. It was comforting and soothed me. As I got older, I still needed that comfort and continued to suck my thumb. My parents were very disturbed at having a seven-year-old daughter who still had this habit. They resorted to techniques like putting hot sauce or castor oil on my thumbs to discourage it. This didn't work and I still couldn't stop despite it, so I did it in private in my room, holding a small piece of the edge of my pillow and smelling it. Looking back I think I yearned to be nurtured. Sucking my thumb calmed my entire body, the sensation of smelling, touching, sucking and holding, all of it was comfort that I was missing from my mum.

Even as I approached my tenth birthday, I continued to suck my thumb while I slept, and eventually my parents consulted a dentist. They were fearful that this would damage the structure of my mouth and force my teeth out. So they resorted to inserting four metal prongs onto my bottom front teeth with the sole purpose of deterring me from inserting my thumb. But the need to suck my thumb was so physically comforting that it overcame my bleeding thumbs from the metal prongs and I endured the pain. I ended up needing braces but Mum and Dad weren't going to waste their money on them if I was going to keep shoving my thumb in my mouth to sleep. No one seemed concerned with figuring out WHY I was still doing it.

As I got older, the need to suck my thumb wore off and I gradually did it less and less, but even when

I was at college if I got upset at something at night, or couldn't sleep, I would self-soothe. I only stopped this behavior when I got married at the age of twenty-four, because I felt great shame at the need to do this comforting act; I didn't want my husband to know that I sucked my thumb.

My parents raised me and my three younger brothers to believe in family. They stressed the importance of hard work and to always do the right thing. For the most part, my brothers and I were very close because we were all each other had. We were always the outsiders in the new towns we moved to, but we never were outsiders to one another.

My brother Patrick was two years younger than me. My dad was very excited at having a son he could share his love of sports and mechanics with. Pat (which he hated to be called) was chubby and awkward at best. He was very fair-skinned, like my parents, and had auburn hair. He had the same blue eyes as both of my parents. His mouth made a little sideways smirk when he lied or if he was antagonizing someone. Pat had girlish attributes and because of this he was teased horribly as he grew up. He didn't care for sports at all and to say my dad was disappointed was an understatement. Dad had played American football and baseball in high school and could have gone on to play them in college if it hadn't been for a career-ending injury. I am sure he wanted his first-born son to carry on his legacy.

Dad was also very mechanically inclined; he was a wonderful handyman and craftsman. He built decks, patios, tore out lawns; there wasn't much he couldn't fix. He also loved to hunt and fish and was a real outdoorsman. Pat however hated the sight of a hammer, as well as the slimy worms he was forced to put on a fishing hook. He couldn't touch them without screaming. He didn't care for playing with his cowboy and Indian toys or cars he got for Christmas. He would much rather play with me and my girlfriends, putting on plays and playing 'house'.

To make matters worse for my dad, my mum recognized this and didn't have a problem with it. For Christmas one year she got me a 'Dressy Betsey' doll and Patrick received a 'Dapper Dan' doll. They were classified as 'educational' dolls and taught children how to tie shoes, zip-up coats and button a jacket. My dad was extremely displeased.

I know that Pat was confused and sad by Dad's attitude because he really liked the doll, From then on he would only play with it when Dad wasn't at home. When my dad did get a glimpse of it I would hear him yell at my mum: 'I thought I told you to get rid of that thing?' She never did.

Pat was also ruthlessly teased about his weight. He

wasn't fat but he had more of a stocky or husky build, while the rest of us were all very slender. The neighborhood kids would chant, 'Patty fatty. Two by four. Can't fit through the bathroom door.' This did a lot of damage in addition to the lack of attention from my dad when he was home. Because of this, Pat and my mum were very close. He enjoyed cooking and she eagerly taught the both of us.

Despite his low-esteem, Pat, like me, had a feisty spirit and because he was teased so much he picked on others to get them back for how he was treated. I suppose it was his way of getting attention and feeling better about himself. When the movie *Grease* was released, he got the soundtrack and sang along to it constantly. He was in love with Olivia Newton John and singing became his vocation. It made him feel in control.

David was the next brother to come along. My mum gave birth to him when she was twenty-four years old, so he was four years younger than me. He came home on Christmas Day wrapped in a red Christmas stocking. He was so tiny he fitted in my baby doll's bed. He looked different than the rest of us, with his olive skin and dark head of hair, though he had the same family trait of baby blue eyes.

David soon became ill. He was unable to hold down any food and rapidly lost weight. Several weeks after being born, he was admitted to hospital for emergency surgery on his stomach and esophagus. He came home a few weeks later with a huge scar across his entire stomach, and thankfully was just fine – much to our relief.

David turned out to be the son my dad didn't have in his first-born and everyone knew it, even Pat. To his credit, Pat has never been angry or resentful at David for this. In fact, I think Pat was relieved that the pressure to live up to Dad's expectations had gone away, knowing he could never measure up. When it became clear that football and DIY weren't for Pat, Dad focused his efforts on his second son. David was diagnosed with hyperactivity when he was ten years old and was constantly getting into trouble. He climbed tall poles meant only for TV technicians and electric workers when he was less than two years old. He would climb up the stairs on top of the railings, not using the steps, and probably would have scaled the walls if his legs had been long enough to reach. My mum couldn't leave him alone for very long for fear of what he would get up to. Several times a day she would ask, 'Where's David?'

One day, when David was four years old, my mum couldn't find him. He was missing for ages. After an extensive search of the house and garden, I found him and yelled, 'Mum, he's in the garage. And you better come here quickly! You have to see this.'

'Oh my,' Mum exclaimed when she entered the garage.

David had taken apart his entire tricycle. Every bolt, screw and tire lay neatly on the garage floor alongside the handlebars, seat and rod.

'David, who did that?' Mum asked him calmly while he stood there with a wrench in his hands from my dad's toolbox.

'Me, of course, silly,' he proudly beamed.

Mum and I were at a loss for words. He couldn't even tie his shoes but he could dismantle an entire trike, piece by piece.

'That's great, honey, but your dad won't be back at home all week. What are you going to do without your trike?' she asked him, still puzzled.

'It's OK, Mum. I'm gonna put it back together!' he said confidently.

Mum just shook her head and went back inside, happy to leave him busy with something to do, knowing where he was and keeping him out of trouble. She figured it would at least keep him occupied for a few more hours, though she didn't fancy a crying four-year-old all week when he didn't have a trike to ride. Never in her wildest imagination would she have thought that he would call us all back into the garage several hours later.

'Ta da!' he said like a magician.

'Oh my,' she repeated, speechless once again.

He had reassembled the trike perfectly.

He loved his trike and his Big Wheel and would go full speed down our steep driveway and then slam on the brakes, sending him flying in circles. He would laugh and walk back up the hill for a second go around. He even tied his trike to our golden retriever to see if he would pull him.

As tough and 'all boy' as David was, he loved to please people and had a heart of gold. He was sensitive, loved animals, wouldn't hurt a flea and loved to make people smile. But by the time he was in his early adolescence, David's teachers and Mum couldn't stand his manic behavior any longer. They put him on a sugar-restricted diet for his hyperactivity, which meant the entire family couldn't have sugar either. No more store-bought cookies, fizzy drinks and sugary breakfast cereals. Mum would drive to Canada and buy liquid artificial sweetener before it was available in the States and started making home-cooked meals. When it was evident that this wasn't working, as he was still as hectic as before, Mum and Dad decided to put him on the hyperactivity medication Ritalin. The life was sucked out of him and he became like a zombie, but when it wore off he'd become a raging maniac. It was hard to see him like that but my parents were being pressured by the school and knew he needed help in order to be able to concentrate on his studies so he could progress.

Michael was born almost exactly two years after David, so he is six years younger than me. When my dad came home from the hospital after my mum delivered him, he said to me, 'Theresa, you have another baby brother.' He knew I had been praying desperately for a little sister.

I was crushed and went to my room to cry. That night, when my mum called us from the hospital, she asked to talk to me. 'You OK, T.T.?'

'Yeah, Mum. It's OK. I will love him too!' I heroically told her with my chin in the air. And I did.

Mike was a cute kid with white-blond hair and the same baby blue eyes as the rest of us. He was filled with mischief. He always made everyone laugh and was super silly. He and Dave got into so much trouble together when they were bored or unsupervised for a long time. They loved to make tents in the room that they shared and once they couldn't find thumbtacks to hold the sheets up so instead they got four-inch cement nails from my dad's workshop and hammered them into the wall. They never did that again after the telling off they received.

Michael was very musical and could play almost any instrument he picked up with grace. He was also extremely smart. He was always thinking of new games to play and ways to make money. He quickly realized that he could profit from other kids' laziness. When his class was assigned with bringing in a current article from the newspaper, he cut out five and on the bus before school he offered the 'extra' ones for a price. On Fridays, when most of the classes had exams, he stocked up on extra pencils and would sell them for a discounted rate compared to the school store and made a huge profit. With the money he made from both endeavors, he would ride his bike to the nearest convenience store and buy large amounts of bubble gum. There were five pieces in each pack and it cost him a quarter – twenty-five cents. He would then sell each piece of gum for a quarter! It wasn't long though before he ended up in the principal's office and they called my mum and dad. My parents were proud of his ingenuity, though, and he didn't get in any trouble at home.

The advantage of having three siblings was that we naturally made two teams for all our games. Pat and David were always a team and Mike and I were a team. It was fair that way since I was the oldest and Mike was the youngest. David was the strongest and fastest and Pat was usually a liability. So it worked out great.

To say that the three of us got into a lot of trouble and mischief when we were young would be putting it mildly. When I was ten years old, we moved to southern Indiana. After being there for just two days, without having fully unpacked yet, Mum decided to take us shopping. 'Come on, kids. We need to go get a new couch.' My mum rounded us all up and we piled into the station wagon. After a short drive, we arrived at a huge furniture warehouse in town.

'Don't touch anything! I mean it,' she said sternly, knowing how we were.

She left to go and talk to the salesman, who seemed distraught at having four young children in his store. 'Let's play hide and seek,' said Michael, championing his favorite game.

'Regular teams!' I declared and we were off and running in seconds. I can't remember who was supposed to find whom, but we had a terrific time in the massive, cement-floored warehouse.

The aisles were filled with tall shelves and new furniture wrapped in clear plastic. Suddenly I saw Patrick speed by me and I took off running. I had been hiding in between some mattresses that were standing straight up on their sides along with metal bed rails. I jumped out from my hiding spot and chased after him. It was a very hot day and I had worn my sandals. They weren't the greatest shoes for running and it felt as if one of my straps had broken as I chased my two brothers. I had to slow down every few steps and shake my foot, hoping to readjust the strap. I saw Mike as he turned the corner towards me.

'Go that way! I saw Pat run that way,' I yelled to him.

But instead of running, he stopped suddenly and his face became ghostly white. 'T.T., you're bleeding!' he cried.

'What are you talking about? No, I'm not! Go after him while I fix my sandal. He is getting away!' I urgently told him.

I bent down to fix my sandal and screamed. There was blood everywhere. My sandal was fine but I had been shaking the pool of blood that had gathered in my sandal every few yards. There now was a trail of blood all the way down the aisle from my hiding spot. I must have unknowingly sliced my heel when I slid out from the mattresses. By now all the boys had gathered to examine my injury. They each took one of my arms and helped me hobble on my foot slowly and gingerly as David, the fastest runner, went to find Mum. 'Mum, T's hurt!' he screamed throughout the store as I limped to the front.

When we found Mum, the alarmed salesman rushed to find a chair for me to sit on. 'Here, young lady. Sit down. Put your foot up here. We need to get it elevated to stop the bleeding.'

'No!' my mum suddenly yelled when he offered me a white upholstered chair.

I knew why she had said that. She had forbidden us to touch anything when we entered the store, knowing how tough four young children could be on furniture. 'I am not allowed to touch anything,' I apologetically told the confused salesman.

My mum, who had had this sort of thing happen many times with four small children, was fast to think and said, 'Where's the nearest hospital? I will take her there.'

As we drove at record speed it felt like Mum was more upset at having her shopping trip cut short and at the prospect of spending the next several hours in a hospital with four kids, than at my injury. 'We haven't even been in town for one week before someone goes to the hospital!' she angrily exclaimed to all of us.

'We won though!' said Mike and I in unison to the other team.

My dad's career really took off when we lived in Indiana and he soon became a skilled salesman, landing several million-dollar corporate accounts. The company discovered he had a talent for taking regional offices that were failing and making them profitable. Once he had turned around one office they would promote him and send him off to the next location that was in the red. He would travel to the offices in his region, work long hours, and be gone for days. He was often required to go to the General Electric headquarters for week-long training sessions he called 'school' and come home only on the weekends, exhausted and just wanting a home-cooked meal. It was the era of large companies and great deals of money. Success and maintaining our lifestyle required my father to constantly accept promotions and transfers.

Mum would resent him being away so much and for being stuck on her own with four young children. When he came home, she just wanted to go out on the town for a meal she didn't have to cook. She was tired of being cooped up with kids all day and wanted to go out and have some fun. But Dad had entertained customers all week and wanted to relax in the big home he had worked so hard to afford. In the end, spending time together as a couple won out and they would go out with friends until early morning. My dad would take my mum along on potential business deals, buy drinks for the entire group and lavish them with expensive meals, while she would smile and be sweet and help him finalize multi-million dollar business deals.

Regardless of how much my dad traveled, he was home every Saturday and Sunday. Even if he was living away from us in temporary housing, waiting for our home to be sold or for us to finish out the school year, he was home for Sunday dinner. We generally went to church every week too, though many times my dad stayed in bed while my mum dragged all four of us to Mass. On Sundays we had two meals, brunch after church and a big dinner in the late afternoon or early evening. We were never permitted to go to friends' houses or do activities on this day because it was a sacred family day but people could come to our house to play. We would watch old movies on TV with our mum as she ironed my dad's shirts and trousers for the coming workweek. I got to iron his handkerchiefs and the tablecloths. Sunday was always a quiet, homey and tranquil day. In the evening, my dad would shine his shoes with the popular news show *60 Minutes* on in the background, and then he would pack his suitcase for the coming week.

We were fortunate that our mother was able to stay at home with us while we were growing up. Even if it was the norm in those days I'm grateful for it. She rarely worked outside the home except on the rare occasions when we needed extra money for braces, college or a trip to Ireland for herself and my grandmother.

Although she stayed at home with us, our lives didn't have a great deal of consistency or stability. I think it takes about one year to settle into a place and another year to adapt and start to fit in. The only consistent things in my life were going to Mass every

Sunday morning, religion classes and our chores, which stayed the same no matter where we lived. Dad loved to make charts and we had a weekly chore chart with our names on it and what jobs we had been assigned that week. They didn't change much. I always had dusting, vacuuming and cleaning the bathrooms on my list. The boys fed the dogs, cleaned up the dog poop, took out the trash and mowed the lawn. We got to team up for dish duty. Mike and I did the kitchen prep with Mum one week, while Pat and Dave were responsible for the clean-up. The next week we switched.

We received a modest allowance on Saturdays for the jobs we had completed in the week. The chore chart served as a reminder of what we had to do and since it was mostly always the same it became a comfort to know it was there. I never liked or understood the division of chores by our gender, but it was consistent and predictable. Sometimes I negotiated a trade with one of my brothers. I wondered how riding the lawnmower while listening to music on headphones and getting a suntan could possibly be considered a chore.

I had so many uncles it was hard to keep their names straight when I was little so I had a special name for all of them. I had a difficult time pronouncing 'grandma' so instead I called her 'Ganno'. Soon my uncles became 'Ganno's boys' and the name has stuck to this day. In Fort Wayne, Indiana, we sometimes went to my grandparents' house for dinner when my dad was out of town for business. Mum got a break when she would go there because there were so many friends and family who would help take care of us.

As I got older, I would stay the night at my grandparents' house. I loved to play in their huge yard, pick peaches and pears off the trees, roll around in the hay bales with the beagle puppies that were being trained to be hunting dogs, or sit by the side of the garden in the early morning, picking weeds while my grandpa worked the land with his hoe. In the evenings, I would see him come back from the law office in his suit and tie, looking stern from a long day of negotiations, but on these mornings he would be dressed in his denim overalls and his face had a peaceful look upon it. Even though he was a successful lawyer and judge, he came from a farming family and never forgot his roots. He went to church every Sunday and helped build a church and made sure in his will that it would be financially supported after his death. He valued family, God and hard work above all else in life. He taught me about nature, how to identify a robin's egg by its blue color and the importance of not touching it otherwise the mother would never return. I learned how to shuck corn by rubbing two ears together and how to throw skeet for my uncles to shoot for target practice.

In addition to building a church, my grandpa also helped start a country club in their town. I spent my summers going to the pool while my entire extended family played golf. Golf was very important in our family and was much more than just a sport. It was a rite of passage. I had my first set of golf clubs in the sixth grade, although I would have much preferred to hang out at the pool with my friends. Travel was also important to my family. My grandparents and uncles traveled overseas regularly, going to Ireland yearly to visit family who lived there. My great-uncle (my grandpa's brother) had moved to Ireland after his wife had passed away so they went to spend time with him. But they traveled all over the world: my grandma would bring me back unique and rare gifts like a koala-fur and kangaroo purses, jade from Japan and wool dresses from Ireland.

In addition to traveling, they were also avid hunters. Grandma would cook anything they killed but she had one rule for all the men in the family: 'If you shoot it, you clean it!' They shot deer and rabbit, pheasant, turkey and geese and afterwards we would sit around having big dinners, eating their prizes while tales of the hunt were loudly shared. During these dinners, many visitors were invited to share in the bounty. It wasn't uncommon to sit next to a senator, judge, monsignor or archbishop. After dinner there would be a fire in the living room and my grandpa would sit in his special leather chair and I would get to sit on his lap as he smoked a cigar and talked with my dad or visitors. It was then that I learned about the law, justice and the Golden Rule: 'do unto others as you would have them do unto you'. The smell of leather, scotch, cigars and firewood burning still brings back special memories.

Sometimes my grandma would get jealous of the extra attention I received from my grandpa. One time she bought me a pair of shiny white boots that I had been begging for. She entered the family room to tell me of my surprise only to discover that Grandpa had already given me the exact pair! Boy was she mad! But not at me. They both showered me with unconditional love, as I was their first grandchild.

When I was seven years old we lived two hours away from our grandparents in South Bend, Indiana. One day when I was at my grandparents' house visiting them, my mum was supposed to come and pick me up but one of my little brothers was sick so my grandma took me to the small airport so I could fly home by myself. 'Theresa, don't be scared,' she reassured me. 'This is your first airplane ride. One of many you will take. It's an adventure! Your mum will be there right when you get off the plane.'

But I wasn't afraid! I loved adventures and was excited to fly.

I was put on a small plane and sat next to a friend of my grandparents who was looking after me. I drank ginger ale and ate peanuts and was having such a good time that I was sad when we landed so soon That night at dinner, my father asked me, 'Theresa, how was your first time on an airplane? Were you scared?'

'It was wonderful, Dad. I had soda pop and saw the clouds and was so close to God's house!' I happily related.

'No one bothered you, did they?' he asked protectively.

'No! Grandma made this nice man, Mr Gates, look after me,' I replied.

My dad looked at my mother. 'Mr Gates? Hilliard Gates, the famous sportscaster?'

'Yes dear, the same one. He is a good friend of the family and was on the same flight,' she explained nonchalantly.

I just nodded and continued to eat my dinner, oblivious to the fact that I had been cared for by a local celebrity. When I think back to this memory I think of how daring I was and how incredible my experiences growing up were. I believed that Ganno's boys would always be there to protect me, and the law would always be on my side.

Someday I would find out just how wrong I was.

One night when I was twelve years old, my mum took all four of us to my grandparents' home for dinner as Dad was out of town for business.

'Hey T.T., why are you so down tonight?' one of my uncles asked.

'No reason,' I lied.

'That's not true!' my brother Patrick chimed in. He could never keep his mouth shut. 'She's upset because a boy at school keeps taking her special erasers.'

'Really? Well you just tell him that Ganno's boys will get him if he teases you any more. OK?'

A sense of relief washed over me. I believed everything my uncles told me, and trusted that they would always be there to protect me.

Soon after, the same boy at school – Scott – started to tease me again. He was pushy and mean and it angered me that he wasn't nice. I couldn't understand why a person would try to hurt someone else. The next day, Scott started to tease me again. 'Hey carrot top. Did you do your homework?' He loved to tease me about my strawberry-blond hair.

'Shut up, Scott! Metal mouth!' I teased back about his braces.

The normally docile male teacher usually ignored our arguing but today he had had enough. 'Scott, Theresa, to the hall!'

We were in trouble. We marched towards the classroom door, our heads hung low. 'Who started it?' demanded our teacher.

'She did!' Scott jumped in first.

'No, he did. He always does!' I stood up for myself.

'Well, I will finish this! I am tired of all your bickering. Go to the principal's office for a spanking!'

I was in shock. I had never gotten in trouble at school and rarely got spanked even at home!

We sat in chairs outside the principal's office for a few minutes until he came out. 'Let's go, you two.' He clearly wanted to get this part of his job over with.

But I defiantly stuck my chin up in the air and firmly said, 'You can't spank me. You have to call my parents first. And if my grandfather finds out, you will be in big trouble! I know my rights!'

The principal stared at me in disbelief then turned back around and went to his office and closed the door. Scott sat there shocked that I had stood up to the principal. 'Are you crazy?' he asked, stunned.

The principal returned. 'Let's go. Scott, in my office. Theresa, you can go back to class.'

I could hear the paddle land on Scott's behind as

I walked back down the hall. He never bothered me again after that day.

That narrowly missed paddling that day taught me an invaluable lesson. That if you speak up for yourself and stand up for your beliefs and what's right, you will succeed. It also didn't hurt for people to know who you were related to. Not getting paddled that day taught me that bullies don't always win. But you have to be stronger than them and stand up for yourself. My family connections rescued me that day but I would forget that important lesson. Had I remembered it, my life would have turned out very differently.

Growing up I overheard heated debates about the law and conversations about business and ethics from my parents and their friends, and the rest of our family. If my brothers and I couldn't agree on something, we had to debate it and offer both sides of the story to my mum who then made the final decision. If there was an argument over which game to play or what TV show to watch, we voted on it and the majority won. We were taught that democracy was an earned right our forefathers had fought for and it was drilled into us never to take that for granted. Voting was not voluntary or an option but a privilege and a responsibility.

As I got older I noticed how goal-oriented and competitive my family was. We loved to play card games, board games, in fact games of any kind and it was just as important to be a good winner as it was to be a good loser. We were taught that being a good sport was one of the most important characteristics to have. My brothers and I also loved to dare one another to do risky things: riding down a steep hill on our bikes, diving off high dives, anything.

We also dared each other to do disgusting things. One day we were making peanut butter and jelly sandwiches for lunch when suddenly one of us dared my brother Pat to make a sandwich that contained a little bit of all the leftovers in the refrigerator and eat it. None of us turned down a dare, so he got out the spaghetti, pickles, a slice of bologna and piled it on and consumed it! This earned cheers from the three of us, and bragging rights for Pat for a long time. On one occasion we went to our favorite ice-cream parlor. The largest item on the menu was the 'Pig's Trough'. It was a gigantic ice-cream sundae made up of nine scoops of ice cream, bananas, strawberries, pineapple, syrups and whipped cream.

'I dare you to get that and eat it all, Patrick,' my little brother David challenged.

'I will even give you five dollars if you do it!' I threw in.

'OK!' Pat agreed. He would do it for the money. To our surprise, he finished every last bite, then got up from the table and ran to the bathroom to throw up. When he returned, he had a huge smile on his face and said, 'Now give me my money!' It was definitely worth my allowance!

Most of our extended family members attended college, worked hard and had successful lives. Much was expected of my brothers and me. It was assumed that I would go to college. The only say I had in the matter was which school I would attend and what would be my major. We were the children of parents who had been expected to make it on their own talent and skill, to become successful without the help or influence of family connections. The same was expected of us.

As I got older I noticed more and more how strained my parents' relationship was. To say their marriage was tumultuous is an understatement. But they hid their unhappiness and tried to bury it with parties, expense accounts, trips and big houses. But no one on the outside had any idea of the turmoil inside our home – how broken it was from the beginning. All they saw was a perfect, happy, successful family living in suburbia.

3

The early years

My family loved to camp. It was my parents' way of
getting away, relaxing and travelling cheaply with
four kids in tow. My dad bought a pop-up camper
that slept eight people and it had a little stove and
refrigerator. He pulled it behind our van and we took
some great trips to Toronto in Canada and Jackson
Hole, Wyoming to see the famous 'Old Faithful'
geyser, buffalo and antelope. My dad and uncle
would go fishing before sunrise in rivers with strong
currents and my mum would cook the fish over the
campfire for breakfast when they returned with their
catch.

We drove to Orlando, Florida to go to Disney World,
to South Dakota to see the presidents carved into Mount
Rushmore, to the Upper Peninsula of Michigan to swim

in the mighty waterfalls, and we went to Mackinac Island where no cars were allowed to drive. We even went to northern New York to see the Thousand Island Lakes, placed bets on racehorses at the tracks and went white-water rafting down fast rapids on the Hudson River. We had a brilliant time camping and making new friends with strangers. Sometimes we would be joined on our trips by our cousins or friends of my parents. Our camping trips were our time to bond as a family. We sang songs, explored, read books and ate wonderful food cooked over the campfire.

During those trips I slept like a baby, lulled to sleep by the noises of the forest. I loved exploring new places with my brothers, learning about history and spending time as a family with no distractions. Back in those days there were no cell phones, portable televisions or laptops so we would play cards on days that it rained. My parents would try to mend their marital problems during the summer, when business was slow and we were off school. All to make us forget the tough year we had had, and the inevitable, upcoming move to yet another unknown city, leaving friends behind and being forced to be the new kids once again.

I always thought my childhood was normal, that surely other people moved a lot too. I think I was just trying to convince myself of this so I didn't feel so lonely. I was allowed to join girl scouts in one place we lived, but then we moved. I participated in sports like baseball in another place, only to stop once we moved again. And I took horseback riding lessons only to move yet again shortly after. The rare occasions when I felt normal were when I was around my extended family. I grew up with twenty cousins and we saw each other every Christmas Eve and every summer at our massive family reunions. Two years in a row, my brothers and I were permitted to attend the same residential Catholic summer camp in Ohio that all my cousins had gone to for years.

It was an odd yet comforting feeling to be able to say, 'this is my cousin', something most kids took for granted. Some kids would even be annoyed with having relatives there as well as them. But I loved it. I got to be the older cousin and look out for them, embracing my maternal side. My younger cousins looked up to me and would boast to their fellow campmates, 'That's my cousin. She is in the senior group!' I desperately wanted to fit in, to be loved, and for someone to notice me.

I first realized that the way I'd grown up was different from others' childhoods when I was eleven years old. I'd befriended a girl with the same first name as me who was bubbly and smiley; everyone loved her. She had an air of confidence about her and I was drawn to her assured nature and positive attitude. She lived in a Victorian-style house in town, a house she had lived in all her life. 'Where did you live before you moved here?' she asked me one day when she had invited me over to her house after school.

'Which time?' I replied.

'What do you mean? Where were you born and where you moved from,' she explained.

'Oh. I was born in Ohio but I have lived in five other places before moving here.'

'What?' She sounded shocked. 'I have lived in my house all my life and I can't imagine ever moving.'

I walked home from her house that afternoon feeling like an outsider, an alien. It was a feeling I knew all too well. I always had to try so hard to be accepted and to fit in. But it was at this moment that I realized something. I came to terms with the fact that this was my life and this was my normal. Even though I'd often daydreamed about not having to move again, I had come to accept my peripatetic life. A smile came to my face as a thought occurred: to me: 'I can't imagine living in one place all my life. How boring!'

I have so many happy memories from my childhood, mostly of the four of us and Mum larking about together. When I was fourteen we went to Florida on a camping trip in the summer holiday. It was the first time my brothers and I had seen the ocean and we searched for seashells, made sandcastles, played in the waves and buried each other in sand.

During the afternoon of our first day at the beach, my brothers were all swimming when Mike suddenly ran past me while I was lying on the sand trying to get a tan. He was screaming and running full speed in the direction of the campground. The rest of my brothers and I ran to the campsite to see what had happened. He had been stung by a jellyfish and was crying loudly in pain.

My mum treated the sting and then told us all, 'Things happen in threes!'

We all looked at one another, shrugged, having heard it many times before, and proceeded to run back to the beach. We wouldn't miss this rare treat of sunbathing, jumping in the waves and searching for shells because of a crazy old saying.

About an hour later, I heard Patrick scream and saw him dashing past me. Shortly before that, he had noticed an older lady swimming nearby, wearing a white swim cap with a pattern of bright flowers on the top. A little while later, he'd reached down into the ocean to pull what he thought was her cap out of the water and return it to her, only to find out it was another jellyfish! As we watched Patrick have medicine applied to his hand and arm, our mum reminded us once again, 'Things happen in threes!'

Now heeding the old saying, David and I slowly looked from one to the other, trying to predict who would be the next victim. 'Looks like it's you or me!' I told him.

We decided that we had had enough of the ocean that day and went to the campground pool instead. It seemed to be a safer choice. We played for hours at the pool where there were a lot of kids, and cute teenage boys. My youngest brother kept begging me to do a flip off the diving board.

'Come on, T. Do a flip! Please?' said Mike.

'I dare you!' Patrick yelled to me.

'OK, but just one,' I replied.

I felt bad for the stings that they had received earlier at the beach and wanted them to be happy, but I was also eager to have a chance to show off in front of the teenage boys. I started by doing a perfect dive off the high board to warm up. Then, after I had everyone's attention, I moved to the low board for the front flip. As I hit the water, I felt very pleased with myself but the momentum from the jump was so strong that my body kept rotating even underwater. I forgot to untuck and the impact of the water caused my knees to slam into my nose. I came to the surface to hear the applause of my brothers and see their smiles, only to feel intense pain. Then the expressions on their faces changed instantly from pride to horror. I looked down and saw the red blood pooling around me as the color of the water changed. I grabbed the ladder and climbed out of the pool, covered my face with my hand and ran for the girls' restroom. I was more embarrassed than anything. I sat down on the floor and my dad came in to help me.

'You can't come in here, Dad!' I objected. I was horrified that he was in the girls' room and even more embarrassed about my face now. He didn't care and helped me clean up – my mum was terrified of blood and would pass out at the sight of it.

The whole family walked slowly back to the camper after that, David, the unharmed brother, with a huge smile on his face. We were done. All three things had happened. Although we decided not to test it again and forwent the ocean and the pool for the rest of the day!

After a fun summer of camping and travelling, I started high school at fourteen years old. We had recently moved to the small town of Flushing, Michigan. About a half mile behind our house was a small pond along with a well-worn trail that led to a bridge over a small creek. We would go swimming, taking peanut butter and jelly sandwiches and bags of chips and spend the entire day there. In the winter, we took our ice skates and a shovel to clean off the snow from the ice and played ice hockey or just skated until we were so frozen that we would be forced to head back to the house for hot chocolate.

Our neighbors had horses, dirt bikes and four-wheeling ATVs and occasionally they would let us go over and play. They had a son called Tommy who was a year older than me and I had a huge crush on him. He was super cute and also had a nerdy sidekick best friend. But of course it was the oddball who liked me! I never seemed to get the popular, cute boys to like me. People commented that I was attractive and nice but I guess I was always an outsider.

School in this new area was different to any other I had attended. The overpopulated school was made up of juniors and seniors, who ranged in age from sixteen to eighteen years old and had school between 7 a.m. and noon, and freshmen and sophomores – fourteen- to sixteen-year-olds – who attended class from 12.30 until 5 p.m. I would see Tommy every day at school because our last names started with the same letter and the lockers were in alphabetical order.

To fill my empty mornings, my mum signed me up for private art classes. My dad was only around at the weekends and Mum already had a close-knit group of friends that she golfed with at the country club and who she'd go out drinking with at the local bar in town called the Speakeasy. The art classes were special to me. Because we moved around so much, we never got the chance to be accomplished at our activities outside school before we were uprooted again. After a while, my brothers and I weren't very dedicated to anything because we knew we would be moving again soon. But art was different for me. I could do it any time, no matter where I lived, and it allowed me to escape deep within the picture I was creating. And my talent for art got me praise and attention from my mother. Something I felt starved of.

Mum was a close friend with Betty, the artist who was teaching me. She had a cool studio upstairs in an old building downtown. One day, after taking me there, Mum stayed during my class. 'Whatcha doing?' I asked her.

'Betty and I are having a private session after you're done. I am having a painting done for your dad for his fortieth birthday present.'

I was fine with that; it had just surprised me that she was staying. I took it in my stride and went to the hamburger shop down the street and then walked to school while my mum was posing for her portrait. A few months later, on my dad's birthday, he opened the present from my mother after dinner and it was a large nude painting of Mum.

'Eww gross!' my brothers exclaimed.

'Boys, it isn't gross. Art is a beautiful thing,' my dad said hurriedly.

'Your father has seen me at my best and he has seen me at my worst. This is somewhere in the middle,' Mum told us.

I think that the portrait was her attempt to bring Dad closer to her and repair their strained relationship. To this day the painting still hangs in their bedroom for everyone who goes in there to see.

One day I was in the kitchen getting breakfast (cold pizza, my favorite) when I gazed out the big window that overlooked the busy country highway in front of our house. Parked on the side of the road was a white van with no passenger windows and two men sitting inside. The driver hung halfway out the window and had a camera with a long lens and was snapping away. He saw me and smiled as a chill washed over my body.

I dropped the pizza and screamed, 'Mum!'

She came running. 'What is it?'

'There are some men taking pictures!' I cried out, pointing to the van at the side of the road. As she looked out the window, the van sped away.

'Maybe it is the property tax assessment company taking pictures of the house for taxes,' she said. 'Go to your room and get ready for school.'

It was still several hours until school but I did as

she said and saw her pick up the phone as I walked out of the room. When I went to the dining room a while later she was still on the phone and I overheard her say, 'OK, Dad. I will.' Then she hung up.

That afternoon after school I told Patrick what I had seen. He was famous for his eavesdropping skills and I knew he would find out what the situation really was. When we all went upstairs for bed that night he reported what he had heard my parents discuss. It turned out there'd been several men who my grandpa had sentenced a few years earlier and who had just been released from prison. They were trying to blackmail him. I wasn't scared, though. I knew my grandpa would take care of it and we were safe. I was confident he and Ganno's boys would always be there to protect me.

Growing up, I always felt very protected. Not by my parents, but by my extended family. It wasn't that I lived in a cocoon. I didn't. I had many opportunities to explore, and travel, and had many extraordinary experiences during my childhood. I felt I would always be taken care of and that someone would always be there to take care of me. But those feelings of security would soon crumble to dust.

Several months later my parents told us that we were moving again.

'But it's March!' I cried loudly. 'It's my birthday

soon and I want to have a party with my friends!'

'Why are we leaving during the school year?' Patrick asked. 'We never do that!'

'Yeah, it's in the middle of my freshman year! I will have to start all over. I will fail!' I cried.

'It's your dad's job,' Mum explained. 'They need us to move again. He's been on the road for several months and he's tired of traveling back and forth from Detroit. He's found a nice house for us there and that's where we are going.'

Something didn't feel right. I was very upset. I was finally starting to fit in and I loved my weekly art classes. To this day I wonder why the move was so rushed. Was it the men in the van with the camera taking pictures? Problems with the church and school? I am likely never to find out the truth to that question.

But that move changed my life, forever.

4

A melting pot

Although it became harder to make friends with every move, each one was also a chance to make a fresh start if I had screwed things up in the last place. But I was really mad about this move, more than any other time. In Flushing, Michigan, I had been in ninth grade and in high school. But in this new town, the ninth grade was still in the junior high school building. I was frustrated that I would have to go back to junior high. I was even more mad that Pat would be in the same school as me again. I had really enjoyed not having my little brothers around me all the time for once.

My dad tried to make it up to us and told us that we each would have our own phones in our bedrooms with a kids' only line. I liked the idea of my own phone but was still disappointed at the thought of going back to middle school. That phone line didn't end up being a benefit.

We moved into an affluent neighborhood in Birmingham, Michigan, a suburb of Detroit. In the 1980s Detroit was a huge, dangerous, thrilling, and exciting city. I got a chance to explore the city on weekend trips with my mother to the farmers' market. Growing up with Midwest farming relatives, I was used to seeing bushel baskets overflowing with fresh-picked green beans, plump tomatoes, and glossy green peppers. But this place was different. Vendors hawked unidentifiable fruits and vegetables from all over the globe. Vast warehouses overflowed with foreign cheeses and teas, scenting the air and enticing me inside every time we visited the market. There were spices and smells even my cultured and worldly mother didn't have a name for.

Dead chickens hung upside down with all their body parts still attached, or a shopper could go around to the back of a building and select a live bird, still clucking, to be slaughtered and cleaned while the shopper waited. In this city a diverse mixture of cultures lived alongside one another. Some groups mixed together in one neighborhood, while unseen street lines divided others. Detroit and its suburbs were dark and dingy one minute and abundantly rich the next. We had moved to the Beverly Hills township of the area. Our town bordered Southfield and half of the kids from this town attended my school.

Just one street separated Birmingham from Southfield, yet the average house in Southfield was valued at $155,000 and whites made up 38 per cent of the population. For the first time, I wasn't in the majority, nor was I one of the richest kids in town. I went to school with a high population of kids who had been born overseas, or whose parents were foreign. This fact would change the rest of my life.

The majority of the high school population consisted of Jewish kids with a large percentage of Chaldeans (Catholic Arabs) and a few Muslim Arabs. On my first day of school I was stunned to see a security guard posted at the end of the school hallway. I had never even talked to a policeman, let alone had one in my school. My only exposure to schools with police, security systems, and metal detectors was from stories of inner-city schools in movies and on television. I was even more astonished to see that none of the other students seemed at all fazed by having a security guard in the building.

I didn't understand why a guard would be in a school for children. I had attended schools in rural areas of Michigan and southern Indiana where classes all but shut down during the fall months because almost all of the boys were hunting with their fathers.

In Birmingham, the school closed on Jewish holidays. I had a total culture shock.

I was accepted into the 'B' group of kids. We were the average kids, second tier to the popular ones. Military brats and other kids who moved around were rarely permitted into the popular group. Slender and well developed for my age with strawberry-blond hair highlighted from perms and time in the sun, I was pretty but not stunning enough for the 'A' group. My clothes were another reason I wasn't permitted to join the popular clique.

As the oldest daughter with three younger brothers, I had a great deal of responsibility. I received a modest allowance for certain approved purchases. Mum didn't approve of brand-name clothing, as she didn't approve of another person's name appearing on my body, so designer labels and make-up were out of the question. Calvin Klein and Gloria Vanderbilt were the rage, but I wore shabby, unbranded clothes. Some weeks I would wear the same item more than once, which I found intensely embarrassing. I wanted to fit in and wear the same chic clothes my friends wore. Household rules dictated that I couldn't shave my legs or date until I was sixteen years old. But what would happen to me before my sixteenth birthday in this place would make all the household rules seem ridiculous and absurd.

*

Making friends at my new school was difficult. I was older than the others and it wasn't the same as starting third grade when everyone wanted to befriend the new kid. They had all known one another since they were small and their parents were all friends. They had extended family close by and took their family vacations the same week of each year, to the same place. They had gone to the same church and doctor all their lives. I couldn't comprehend this way of life. I was jealous of the predictability and stability of it, while on the other hand, they were jealous of my nomadic and adventurous way of life.

My mother thrived in our new home. She embraced the multicultural aspect of our new home. We attended ethnic festivals downtown, sampled unusual food, sat on the cement steps of the outdoor theater and watched the cultural events that took place there. People proudly wore the costumes of their native countries and danced as if it were a hundred years ago. Mum opened our home to cultural exchange students from other countries, giving them a bed and family to live with while studying. Eventually she took a position with the local exchange student chapter to help find families for students coming here from abroad.

Mum's other endeavor in our new home was Birmingham's community theater. She auditioned in the small playhouse and rehearsed upcoming roles. She was good. While my father was away on business, it gave her something to do. Mum joined the Gourmet Club, a group of four couples who each month would decide upon a country as the focus of a dinner. The women discussed the menu, one couple provided the main course, and another researched the music, drinks, and decorations. An adult-only occasion, my dad was an eager participant, enjoying getting away from work to appreciate good food with friends.

Although my brothers and I were enlisted to peel twenty pounds of shrimp, or help in the preparation of their meal that we wouldn't get to eat, we didn't complain much. We were used to being shooed to our rooms while our parents' friends came over. We made our own party of it with salty treats that were generally off limits to us, soda, and samples from the dinner they were making. We spent the evening watching our favorite movies such as *The Wizard of Oz* or *Chitty Chitty Bang Bang*. Sometimes I told stories to my brothers or read them books. They loved adventures like *Robinson Crusoe*, mysteries such as the *Hardy Boys* and Disney books as long as they weren't too girly.

Dad's job required a great deal of entertaining in our home and in public, so I was taught to be well behaved when others, particularly Dad's co-workers and sales clients, were around. I learned how to carry on conversations with adults on a multitude of topics. I didn't know in-depth amounts of any particular subject but just enough to hold an intelligent conversation.

When the party went on late into the night and my brothers got bored, they would make tents out of bed sheets hanging from the furniture. Heads hurting from a long night of partying, our parents wouldn't check on us until late the following morning. By that time I had cleaned up our mess, making sure not to anger them.

My mum wasn't a morning person. As she didn't work outside of the home, she stayed up late at night, shut away inside her room when my dad was gone, and slept in late in the mornings. If my dad was home, he would wake us all up and we would get ready for school by ourselves. Typically, I helped my brothers tie their shoes or get dressed. My dad is colorblind so each morning he would call me into his closet to help him find a tie that matched his suit for the day at the office. Mum slept soundly as the rest of the house got ready for the day. We would go downstairs and my dad ate breakfast and read the newspaper before leaving for work.

'Theresa, there is some nice grapefruit on the counter. Have some breakfast,' he'd say.

'Dad, I hate breakfast. You know that,' I'd mutter.

I would busy myself packing four lunches for school: peanut butter and jelly sandwiches or bologna, plastic baggies full of potato chips, some homemade cookies and that was it. We rarely got to buy a hot lunch at school and had to make do with a cold sandwich.

Life then wasn't like it is today. Children looked after themselves more and weren't as mollycoddled. Children weren't into multiple activities; our parents didn't shuttle us to games and practices. We didn't sit around the kitchen table doing our homework together. Each of us chose one activity, usually scouts, and rode our bikes if we wanted to go somewhere. Mum wasn't about to take us to the mall just because we were bored. My brothers delivered newspapers and worked together the evening before to wrap them up and then rode their bikes the next morning at the crack of dawn to deliver them. They made good money and enjoyed being active.

One afternoon, when I was fifteen years old, I was sitting in the family room watching a TV show and doing my homework. My brother David came into the room. He was eleven years old and always in trouble or up to something. He had his beige-colored, cloth newspaper carrier bag over his shoulder and sat on the floor next to me. 'T, I got you something,' he said proudly, barely able to contain his smile.

'What is it?' Knowing him, it could be anything from a rock to a plastic ring from a gumball machine. But I loved any surprise or gift.

He dumped out the contents of the carrier bag and out rolled a little black-and-tan puppy! I screamed with excitement.

The puppy was beautiful. He had a white cross emblazoned on his chest and he scared himself when he tried to bark. We'd had to leave one of our dogs at the old house before we moved because we didn't have a garden big enough for him, so my parents agreed to let us keep this puppy. David had used some of his newspaper money and bought him from someone at the park. I named him Bowzer after one of our favorite singers in a 1950s tribute group called Sha Na Na. Bowzer went with us everywhere and we got compliments on his unique markings when people passed by.

My brothers and I were very active. We would be gone all day long riding our bikes, going to the park, the private swim club we belonged to, the fast-food restaurant at the corner, the drug store, and the library. I adapted to the new town and the new way of life as best I could. My grades in school were average. I didn't excel at anything in particular. I was pretty, but not beautiful. Average-sized, but not skinny. I was in choir but didn't have solos. Because I was lonely, making new friends and being accepted became extremely important to me.

In the summer following my freshman year of high school when I was fifteen, my parents bought a membership to the private community pool near our house. This was unusual because they usually joined the local country club so they could golf but would never join the pool. Getting up at 7 a.m. to go play golf for a few hours during my summer breaks was not my idea of a good time, especially when I passed all my friends having fun at the pool. But here we could ride our bikes down the street to the pool and wouldn't pester Mum all summer long with nothing to do. I was still really angry at having to go back to junior high in the middle of my freshman year so I think this was a way to make it up to me for the move.

At the pool, I worked on my tan, read historical romance novels and swam. Usually by mid-afternoon, one of my brothers would bug me to do a dive off the high board. 'Come on, T.T. Go off the high dive. Please?'

Whenever I started to say no, Patrick would say, 'I dare you, T!' He knew I would give in if they dared me.

I enjoyed diving and swimming and always felt free and at peace in the water. Plus I liked the extra attention I got when I dove off the high dive. 'All right, just once though,' I'd say as I adjusted my skimpy green bikini and walked around the pool towards the board. I wasn't oblivious to the male heads that turned as I strolled by. After my dive, I'd leave the pool to my brothers' applause. 'That's my sister, Theresa. She's in high school,' they would tell their friends. It was so easy to please nine- to thirteen-year-old boys!

Occasionally I noticed some dark, olive-skinned young men at the pool. However, I never saw any Middle Eastern girls. When the men and boys were there, they would spend the entire time staring at me. It made me very uncomfortable. They would talk loudly in a foreign language as I passed by and often they tried to get me to come over to them. It scared me and I would shake my head 'no' and keep walking, trying to ignore their jeers.

That summer my parents took us on another camping trip with friends of the family and we spent a day on a friend's massive yacht at a popular lake island retreat. I met Jim on Lake Erie at Put-in-Bay, Ohio. He was two years older than me and he soon became my first real boyfriend. He lived several hours away in a suburb of Cleveland, Ohio, and we wrote letters and talked on the phone every day. Jim and I had big dreams. Our love knew no limits. It was an innocent, love-at-first-sight relationship and it felt like nothing could separate us, not even distance. We planned to go to prom together and one day to get married. We both were from Catholic families so had seriously discussed sex before marriage and agreed to wait until our wedding night.

My parents didn't like the fact that Jimmy was older than me. They said that it would be best for me if I dated other boys. I, of course, balked at this but as a dutiful daughter agreed for the sake of keeping the peace. We were still permitted to date but my parents were sure that we didn't stand a chance of making it due to our age and distance.

That summer I also discovered how much I loved to tan. I would gather up a big beach towel, a bottle of baby oil with iodine added to get a deeper tan, and lemon juice to put on my hair to make it blonder. I'd put on my bikini and trot to the backyard with my belongings. I would get all ready to relax but within minutes Mum would find me and insist that I come inside for some urgent chore that needed to be done immediately. Begrudgingly, I would pack it all up and head back inside.

I wasn't a stranger to attention from boys and men and this felt so good because I didn't get a lot of that kind of affirmation at home. I was taught that good looks were not of value or importance and that it was a sin to be vain. My brothers teased me for having 'thunder thighs' but I managed to feel pretty due to the attention from boys. I don't think I was ever told 'you look beautiful' by my parents, even to this day. Was it any wonder, then, that when a handsome older boy told me those words that I became fascinated with him?

My high school's homecoming dance was scheduled soon after I began the new school. It was my first dance and I was asked to go by a quirky boy with big fuzzy hair and even bigger glasses. He was a nice, quiet Jewish boy, somewhat shy, but I was happy to have a date and fit in for a change. The downside of moving a lot was that I was always the new girl and all the cute, popular boys were already taken. I got stuck with the nerdy, quiet boys with low self-esteem who were so amazed that I had accepted their approaches that they ended up not talking to me much.

'Mum, I need to get a new dress for the dance,' I casually mentioned one afternoon.

'Theresa, you have plenty of dresses that are good enough,' she said, clearly not interested in paying for new clothes for me.

'But Mum, I wore the purple dress already and haven't had a new outfit for a long time.'

'You just got new clothes for school in August. No one has seen that dress and it still fits fine. The answer is no.'

I stormed out of the room and ran to my bedroom and cried. I ultimately went to the dance in the purple dress, but I wasn't happy about it. A picture of the Jewish boy and me dancing appeared in the school's yearbook. Although I don't think we ever spoke again after the dance, we exchanged smiles as we passed each other in the school halls.

I made a few friends and on weekends we went to the high school football games, sometimes sneaking in small amounts of vodka from our parents' liquor cabinets to be cool. I had never drunk alcohol before. It made me feel important to be able to drink with my friends. And the effects of drinking small amounts of liquor made me feel as if I was one of the girls. I was more concerned with fitting in than how the alcohol made my body feel. I went to the movies, had sleepovers, and frequently went to the local ice-cream parlor with my friends. Sometimes I felt the kids were letting me hang out with them, as if they were doing me a favor. They had accepted another girl into the group the year before who was a military brat. No one really liked her but I suppose they figured if they let her in they should let me in as well. Regardless of the reason, I was determined to make the best of it, as I had done so many other times. Until we would be told to pack up the boxes again and move to the next place.

All my new friends dressed in very expensive clothing and had the newest styles featured in the magazines we read so avidly. But my mum hated shopping. Even though my dad bought her the best, most elegant outfits, and he had a huge walk-in closet full of designer suits, hundreds of ties and top-of-the-line dress shoes, us kids received clothes once a year when we went back to school, and the most I was allowed to spend was $100. My mum would say, 'You can choose to buy one pair of designer jeans with that money or a bunch of "no brand" things. Why would you want someone else's name on your butt anyway?'

I ultimately chose the low-cost clothes and had a few outfits I wore each week. It was embarrassing especially since I lived in a big house and we belonged to the country club. I ended up wearing the purple dress for three homecoming dances and also for my graduation pictures and the same formal gown for two proms and a cotillion in four years. Mum also didn't like me to 'primp' too long and would complain if she thought I spent too much time in front of the mirror getting ready. 'You will become vain if you spend any more time in the bathroom Theresa,' she would say angrily. 'Come on, let's go now.'

I was fascinated by the Arab culture, which was so prevalent in my school and community. The more I learned about it, the more intrigued I became. This was a culture of people thrown out of their country years before due to religious persecution. Chaldeans are a minority within the Iraqi population due to their religion, Catholicism. Iraqi Christians compose a mere 3 to 6 per cent of the population in Iraq. Arabic in ethnicity, yet of the Christian religion, they practice the Catholic faith. While living in Iraq and the surrounding predominantly Muslim countries, Chaldeans were forced to leave their home in order to survive and keep their Catholic faith. Chaldeans immigrated to America in the early 1900s, encouraged by Middle Eastern immigrants already here. Michigan became a location of choice for Chaldeans because it was one of the few states that still permitted first cousins to marry one another. Marrying within their family network is common, if not expected.

Most of the students I went to school with were first-generation American born, yet some of the older students had a slight accent when they spoke. They spoke Arabic at home and English at school. Fascinated, I wanted to befriend this group to find out more about them. I thought we had quite a bit in common. First, we were all Catholic. Though some had their own Chaldean Catholic churches, many attended the same church as I did. Secondly, similar to Irish culture, they had strong family ties. But it was the differences between us that really interested me. In my Irish heritage, the people are mostly fair-skinned and light-eyed. Material items aren't generally of value, and women and men are equal partners in life. In the Chaldean culture, women keep to themselves; girls are confined to their own groups at school and at church. They didn't get involved in after-school activities, going straight home after class each day. Closely watched by the male Chaldeans, mostly relatives, the girls were secluded, quiet, and demure. Families followed traditional roles differentiated by strict gender lines. I found this all quite scary but also very exciting.

As I examined this group of people I was immediately drawn to a handsome Chaldean boy named Daniel. Even though he was in the same grade as me, he seemed several years older. He drove a car at the beginning of our sophomore year when the rest of us were just turning fifteen and the legal age to drive was sixteen. I thought he must have been at least two years older than me. He had jet-black hair, dark eyes, olive skin, and a beautiful smile. He dressed impeccably in crisply pressed Ralph Lauren shirts and slacks. He wore gold jewelry: a thick gold bracelet and a long, gold rope chain with a little camel charm that hung from it. This was typical of most Arabs in my school. He also smelled wonderful from his generously applied designer cologne.

Daniel worked part-time in the school's student store. Every time I noticed he was working, I'd go in and buy an eraser or a pencil. He was attentive when I was around. I knew he was attracted to my blond hair, creamy white skin, and feisty spirit. My girl-friends warned me about him. 'You're off limits,' they told me. 'You aren't Chaldean. He could never date you. Don't even think about it.' I didn't listen.

My family valued culture and diversity. My grand-father assisted immigrants with legal problems and my parents sponsored international students who lived with us from time to time. My boyfriend, Jimmy, was Italian-American. I had attended several school dances with Jewish boys. In my previ-ous schools, boys tolerated girls and teased them. Most of the guys were heavily involved in sports, outdoor activities like four-wheeling, skating, and racing. They helped their dads on the farm or at work. Young good ol' boys in the making. It was dif-ferent in Birmingham where the boys were suave, well dressed, and smelled good. They passed me in the halls, looked me over with an enticing smile on their faces. These boys didn't know what it was like to work outside in the cold or go hunting. Their fathers owned their own stores or businesses. They were making money and taking everything from life that they could.

The attraction between Daniel and me grew stronger each day. I liked him for his differences. He was exotic. I suppose he liked me too, though at the time I wasn't sure. In addition to the physical attraction, an air of being off limits to each other added excitement. He would stop me in the hall sometimes and tell me I looked pretty that day. I could feel his eyes staring at me the entire lunch period from across the room. He would pass closely by me when we changed classes and brush up against me. And sometimes he would offer to help me with my heavy load of textbooks, though I always declined.

In Daniel's culture, women were of a lower status. Young men were taught not to respect women or take no for an answer. I wasn't used to this and didn't understand it. My mum ran the house, supervised the children and ran all the finances. My parents taught us that we make our own destiny and that we were all equal. My brothers weren't even allowed to hit me in a playful manner because they were taught to respect women. I couldn't accept that people living around me were treated so unjustly but I was interested in their different values.

By the spring semester, I was struggling with my grades. The district's strict academic standards were different from those in rural settings where teachers were glad you showed up and hoped you were wearing shoes. Daniel and I continued eyeing each other up while boys in my own league failed to pursue me. Jim and I wrote letters and planned my upcoming birthday and his prom in the spring. We were competitive letter-writers: he would write five pages to me one day and I would write six back. Then he would write seven. For Valentine's Day, he sent me a four-foot-tall Hallmark card. I was shocked when the mailman delivered it and happy for the attention and love I received from Jim on a daily basis.

We were so different, from two different ways of life. Jim was from a small, working-class family from the city. To his family, being a good person was more important than how much money you made or your accomplishments in life. Having a family, wife, children and going to church on Sundays were what made a person of good quality. Being dependable and trustworthy and having enough to provide for your family and sitting down to large family dinners was more important than paying your bills.

My family stressed the importance of accomplishments and rising to the top of your class and having a profession, not a job. Where you went on vacation, what kind of car you drove and how many bathrooms your house had were important. As was seeing family on special holidays, but making it on your own and being independent, paying your dues and expecting everyone to contribute to life was of huge importance to our parents.

Even though me and Jim saw the similarities in each other, I think we were drawn to the differences. And the desire we each had for what the other took for granted.

I loved Jim's family's unconditional love and acceptance of who you were right at that moment, not focusing on your potential. I felt strongly about serving others with no expectations of receiving anything in return. I think Jim loved the ambition to be more than just a blue-collar worker that he felt when he was around my family. He dreamed of more than just providing for his family; he also saw that he could have a career.

Yet we would get into arguments regularly because he felt a duty to provide for me the lifestyle that I had become accustomed to. And I would argue with him that this wasn't what I wanted. I wanted the security and strength that emanated from his family and didn't care about riches.

Jim's prom was fast approaching so – unusually – Mum took me to a mall to shop for my prom dress. I selected a baby-blue floor-length satin gown with white, sheer lace. I was also allowed to buy a baby-blue satin suit with pants and vest with the allowance money I had saved up. They were the first chic, stylish clothes I owned. My parents let me plan my

Sweet Sixteen birthday party. It would be held in our recently refinished basement. We had a pool table and I was planning to move my stereo down there too. Now I would definitely fit into the cool group.

In February, the high school announced tryouts for the track team. I had been on the track team at my previous school and wasn't half bad. We practiced after school every day, doing drills in the gym due to the frigid Michigan weather. I had more freedom, staying after school every day and going home later in the afternoon.

Two Chaldean boys, Bassim and Hassam, sat behind me in speech class. They both spoke broken English with strong accents. Dressed in simple clothing, without cologne, and wearing small gold jewelry, they weren't the same as the other super-confident Chaldean boys. Cousins from a lower-middle-class family, they were considered black sheep. Passing back their graded papers, I knew they were having difficulty in class and I befriended them because I knew they needed help. I also wanted to find out more about their culture.

When I got my driving license, my parents purchased an old 1972 Ford Torino I nicknamed Dino after the dinosaur. Far from pretty, the brown, two-door with burgundy leather interior was my key to freedom. To pay for my freedom, I took a part-time job at the Burger King at the end of the street. The kids who worked there hung out together after work. During the day, Birmingham was an upper-middle-class neighborhood with large homes, flower-lined streets, and grassy parks. When the sun went down, the same streets became dangerous.

One night, I went out with a girlfriend who was Jewish. I drove to the Burger King to say hello to my co-workers and see if there were any leftovers. Pulling into the parking lot, I saw a commotion in the drive. Two groups of kids faced each other. Fists raised, they screamed profanities at one another. They swung sticks connected by a chain. 'Those are nunchucks,' my friend explained. 'The guys use them for fighting. Especially the Arabic and Jewish boys.'

Suddenly the boys flung the weapons at each other. Everyone was running, falling to the ground, and bleeding. I turned the car and sped away.

'It's a turf fight,' my friend explained.

'You mean like in those 1950s movies?' I was shocked.

'It is Arab boys fighting Jewish boys. Other towns are strictly divided and only one or two types live there. But here, because of the money, many rich kids from different backgrounds live in the same neighborhood and go to the same school. At night, they fight for power.'

The sight of their spilt blood stayed with me. I told my parents what I had seen and my mum compared it to the political, religious and cultural situation in Northern Ireland, where people fought for something that had started many years ago but continued to do so as it had become a way of life. My dad set new rules that included me staying closer to home after dark.

Power and control set the tone for the entire city, no matter what part you lived in. People knew who had the power by what kind of convenience, grocery, or liquor stores were in the area and whose last name was on the signs. Another indicator was the type of churches, mosques, or temples in the area. Within our church, there were Chaldeans and others. We attended the same school, yet were divided when we congregated at the church. We sat on different sides and did not mingle, not even for fundraisers or festivals. I sometimes wondered if we really even shared a common bond of religion.

Shortly after homecoming, I befriended a classmate from my English class named Ana. She was a foreign exchange student from Brazil. We were talking one day during class and she confided in me, 'Theresa, do you know anywhere I can live for a few months?'

'What happened? Don't you live with Sue and her family?'

'Yes, but my host family doesn't want me to live

there anymore. They want me to clean their house, help cook and do my own laundry. I don't want to do that so they said I have to find a new family.'

Ana's parents were diplomats from Brazil and she had grown up with servants who did all the work. She had never cooked a meal or washed a dish in her life.

'Let me ask my mum if she knows anyone,' I offered.

That night I explained Ana's situation to my parents and they agreed to let her stay with us for the rest of the semester until it was time for her to return home. Mum was still working with the company for international students and was really enjoying it. She volunteered with them at first and then eventually began to work part-time for them finding students good homes.

I was happy to finally get a sister, even if it was only temporary. Ana had her own room at our house, a converted den room. We took her on camping trips to Niagara Falls and she grew to like America. She was quiet and unconfident in her language skills but loved living with our big family. Right before she returned home at Christmas, she gave my mum a massive seven-carat amethyst stone. 'My dad wants you to have this as a thank you,' she told my mum. That stone was later put into a high school gradu-ation ring for me, designed by one of my uncles in the jewelry business. (Years later, I ended up pawning it for grocery money when things were rough. It was opulent, awkward and I felt uncomfortable wearing it. I needed milk and nappies more than a ring I never wore that had sat long forgotten in the back of my jewelry box.)

Life was so different here and there was so much to take in. It was all quite a culture shock. Little did I know what was lying in store for me in this crazy, exhilarating yet totally alien environment.

5

Changed forever

My long conversations with Jim were always tying up the home phone for hours and Mum didn't like the fact that she couldn't receive calls. The perk when we moved again was that each of us had our own private line in our bedrooms so I could talk to Jim without getting in trouble for holding up the line.

Late one evening I was watching television with my family when the phone rang on the main house line. My mum went to answer it and returned with a scowl on her face. 'Theresa, phone,' she said. 'Get rid of those Arabs right now.'

Confused, I went to the nearest phone in the hall. 'Hello?'

'Theresa, this is Daniel, from school. I work in the school store.'

Like I didn't know who he was. 'Yes?'

'Look, I need to talk you ...'

My mum was standing next to me. 'Get rid of them, Theresa,' she repeated. 'Right now!'

'But he's from school. He has a question about homework,' I lied. I was flattered that he'd called me. I heard other voices in the background. 'Theresa. How's it going, baby?' I couldn't place this new unfamiliar voice on the line. But I could see my mum getting angry. 'I gotta go,' I hurriedly said. 'Bye.'

My mum took the receiver and slammed it down. 'We don't accept calls from Arabs at this house,' she stated firmly.

'They aren't Arabs, Mum,' I responded, defending them. 'They're Chaldeans.'

'I don't care who they are. They won't be calling here anymore, do you understand?'

I nodded, a bit confused at her response. Her reaction seemed unusual for her. She was usually so open to other cultures. Was she upset because a boy was calling me or because he was foreign? I didn't know why she was so angry. All I could think about was that Daniel had called me. My mind started to race. How did he get my number? Oh well. It didn't matter, he had called me.

The next day at school, it was hard not to tell my friends that Daniel, the gorgeous Chaldean, had called me at home. But I kept it to myself, going from class to class with a smile on my face. Approaching the cafeteria at lunch time, I realized I had left my lunch in my locker. 'Hey, guys, I gotta run back to my locker,' I told my friends. 'I'll be right back.'

I walked to the opposite end of the high school, past the security guard who was perched on his stool reading a book, turned the corner and headed to my locker. Concentrating on the locker combination, I didn't hear anyone approach. As I found the last number of the combination and pulled open my locker, a hand reached up and slammed my locker door shut.

'Hello there, Theresa.' It was Daniel's two older cousins. What were their names? These guys were in a grade above me but I knew that they were much older than the typical age of a junior in high school, sixteen or seventeen years old. They seemed to be at least eighteen, had a heavy accent and had an air of danger to them.

'Hi,' I said tentatively, feeling fearful.

'Do you know why we are here?'

'I have no idea,' I responded, confused.

They laughed and chills ran up my spine. With one hand resting on my closed locker door, one of the cousins (the shorter one) leaned dangerously close, his face just inches from mine. 'You hung up on us last night. We don't like it when people hang up on us.'

'I wasn't talking to you. Daniel called me. My mum hung up the phone because I am not allowed to talk to boys.'

'Well, you hung up on us,' the older, quiet one accused.

'No,' I insisted, not knowing why I was trying to convince them. 'I said goodbye before I got off. It wasn't my fault. It was my mother.'

The shorter, stouter cousin closed the gap between us and stood inches away from me. The second cousin backed me against my locker. 'Don't ever hang up on us again.'

As I nodded, he spat in my face. Saliva covered my eyes and forehead and ran down my face, over my nose, my mouth, and chin. They walked away, laughing.

Shaking, I wiped the thick spit from my face and tried to compose myself. I was afraid that someone had witnessed this humiliation. The halls were usually a busy place. Now they were oddly empty. I forgot about my lunch and walked past the guard who had done nothing. He kept his eyes down, pretending to read his book. Pretending he hadn't seen what had just occurred. I was stunned not only by their crude, disgusting action, but also by the unresponsive guard. It was his job to protect people and he had simply refused to get involved. He was the first of many who would turn their back on me. This I think was due to an overwhelming sense of fear, even when a child was involved.

When I returned to the cafeteria, lunch was nearly over. 'Where have you been, Theresa?' my friend asked.

'I was in the bathroom. I don't feel so good all of a sudden. I'm going to call my mum and go home sick.'

At home, I told my mum I had cramps and ran water in the bathtub. I eased into the warm soothing waters. I had been violated and felt dirty. I had been taught that spitting was the dirtiest thing a person could do. It was low class and degrading to do it to another person. And I still did not understand why they had done that to me.

My parents agreed to let me have a boy-girl party for my Sweet Sixteen birthday. I planned it for months and hoped it would make my friends like me more, that it would make me more popular. There were still many inside jokes that I wasn't privy to and sometimes they made plans and went places without me. We had just remodeled our basement and I had painted modern designs on the wall around the billiards table. I requested my mum make my favorite cake, Angel Food with pink icing. I even made a poster board for everyone who came to the party to sign so I could remember the day forever. I desperately wanted Jim to come from Cleveland but we were planning to go to his prom in May and he couldn't afford a bus ticket for my birthday party as well as all the prom expenses. I tried to understand, but I was disappointed. My friends were beginning to wonder if he was real.

I invited all my friends and their boyfriends or the guys they had crushes on. I really wanted to invite Daniel, the adorable Chaldean boy. Every time I looked, he seemed to be around. I asked my friends what they thought about me inviting him to the party. 'Are you crazy? They don't come to white people's parties!' was the response.

'I don't think I've ever seen one at a dance either,' another friend replied.

'Or even at a football game,' someone else chimed in.

Well I didn't care. I had a massive crush on him, even though I had a boyfriend. Jim lived so far away and my parents had stressed to me that I needed to date other boys. My heart dropped into my stomach every time I saw Daniel or he said 'hi' to me in the hall in that sexy, slightly accented voice.

After a few days of contemplation, I mustered the courage to write him a note.

Daniel, I'm having a Sweet Sixteen birthday party on Saturday, March 21st. Will you come? Theresa.

During lunch, I walked into the student bookstore where he worked. I waited until no one was looking. I couldn't help but be aware of his intense gaze that had followed me ever since I walked in the door. I found the cheapest thing I could buy and took it to the register. Without saying a word, I paid for the pencil and handed Daniel a folded up note and ran out of the store.

I knew my friends didn't want me to invite him but I desperately wanted him to come. I was going to be sixteen, a woman, and finally be allowed to date properly, shave my legs, and wear make-up without hiding it anymore. I felt like all my dreams would come true when I turned sixteen. My party was in six weeks' time and I dreamed that maybe Daniel would come and kiss me on my birthday. Little did I know that more than that would soon happen to me.

On a cold February day, after school, I rushed to the gym locker room to change into my track uniform for practice. The uniform for gym class was a one-piece jumper: solid blue shorts and a striped blue and white top that zipped together. It was polyester, extremely ugly and uncomfortable. I was waiting for the other girls to arrive when I realized I had forgotten some books in my locker that I needed to take home so that I could study them that evening. I ran down the hall, using it as an excuse to warm up. As I turned the corner, I was amazed to see Daniel. Who else's locker was near mine? Who could he be looking for? Surely not me. My heart dove into my stomach and started to beat even faster than I knew it should from the brisk, sudden run.

'Do you want a ride home?' he asked.

I couldn't believe he was talking to me. Before my brain had a chance to even think about it, my mouth had responded. 'Sure, practice just got cancelled,' I lied. 'I just need to get my coat.'

Anything to get to spend time with him without the watchful eyes of my disapproving friends. I went by the gym, grabbed my things and told the coach that I didn't feel well all of a sudden and was going to go home.

Daniel and I walked to the school parking lot to his new black Pontiac Trans Am GT. It was an expensive, sporty car that not many high-school boys could afford. I hurried to get inside so my running mates wouldn't see me leaving practice with him.

Daniel drove out of the school parking lot and turned the wrong way.

'I live the other way,' I told him, alarmed.

Daniel gave me a beautiful smile. 'I know, Theresa. But I want to spend some time with you and get to know you better. I have wanted to do this for a long time. But I need to run by my house first to get something. I'll take you home after that.'

I was too blinded by his charming demeanor to realize that he wasn't really asking for my permission. How could I say no? Here was the guy I had had a crush on all year long and he wanted to spend time with me. I was too naive to be scared.

Daniel pulled into the driveway of a huge house. There were no other cars in the driveway. Alarms went off in my head, as no one else seemed to be there – did this mean I was going to be alone with him? But I thought I knew him so I trusted him. It's not like anything is going to happen, I thought to myself. After all, I have a boyfriend who I'm going to marry after I graduate.

I justified everything and ignored the red flags. Daniel and I had had stolen moments to talk. Little chats in the hall, at my locker, and in the store. He had asked me if I had a boyfriend and I had hesitantly told him yes. We attended the same Catholic church, though more often it was his sisters and female family members who came. He was Catholic and I assumed that he knew I had the same values and morals as were stressed in the church teachings.

'I need to run inside,' he said. 'Do you want to come with me?'

'No. I'll wait here. My mum is waiting for me at home,' I said nervously.

Daniel turned to me and put his face close to mine. 'Theresa, I like you.'

My heart stopped. I definitely didn't want to sit and wait in the car now. And I was interested in seeing the inside of his home. I had heard many rumors that 'outsiders' were rarely permitted inside Chaldean homes and it appeared to be big enough to house many families. I thought everything would be fine.

Inside, Daniel showed me around the house.

'Where is everyone?' I asked. I was used to my mother and brothers being home when I got back from school every day.

'Don't know,' he hedged. 'They should be home any minute, though.'

The house was stunningly decorated. Rich-colored rugs hung everywhere. Gold-framed pictures and candlesticks abounded. It smelled like incense at Mass on holy days. Following him upstairs, more warning alarms sounded in my head.

'We should get going, Daniel. My mother will be expecting me,' I said, lying again. She thought that I was where I was supposed to be, at track practice. Not for a moment would she be sitting at home thinking that I was with this cute Chaldean guy in his family's home. If I couldn't talk to him on the phone, I knew I would never be permitted to go to his house.

'Just a few minutes, Theresa. I want to spend some time with you,' he pleaded. 'You like me, don't you? I have always liked you a lot.'

I should have known better but his sweet voice coupled with my desire to be special to him lured me into staying. From the mini-refrigerator in his bedroom, he pulled out a can of something cold. With his back to me, he poured the liquid into a glass and handed it to me. It tasted strange. Bitter. Perhaps it was the odd smells of the house, the incense or maybe it was the soap they used to wash the glasses, I thought to myself.

We sat on his bed and my heart sped up with the knowledge that he was going to kiss me. I was feeling dizzy, not sure whether it was because I was so excited at the thought of him kissing me or if I was getting sick. I had daydreamed of this moment for a long time. I thought of Jimmy but I knew a kiss was harmless. After all, I was young and my parents said they wanted me to date others before I settled down with one guy.

Daniel leaned in and kissed me. He was older and I could tell from the kiss that he was experienced. I was fifteen years old and a virgin but I was longing to be accepted and loved. We kissed for a long time, then things began to progress. I had had more experience in petting than I care to admit now, but I always knew when to stop. I enjoyed the attention boys gave me, but I was a good Catholic girl. My head reeled under Daniel's caresses. Or could it have been from the drink? Daniel's hands began roaming, distracting me as he unzipped my track uniform and attempted to tug it down to my knees. Alarms sounded anew in my brain and I knew I had to tell him to stop. I knew right where that line was.

'I want you now.' His voice was muffled against my flesh, his hands insistent.

'No, Daniel! You have to stop now! I need to go home.' Daniel ignored my wishes. 'Daniel! I mean it. I have to go. My mother will be worried about me,' I pleaded.

Still not even an acknowledgment from Daniel. Panic crowded my throat. No one had ignored me before. Boys always stopped when I told them to. They had always respected my wishes and stopped. My head began to pound and my body was hot. I was feeling sick.

'Theresa, please. I want you so badly.'

I didn't want to do this. I was waiting until I was married to give my virginity. And I had already promised it to one certain boy.

'Daniel, I'm a virgin. **Please** stop now!'

My head was spinning. I was terrified. With my hands against his chest, I pushed with all my strength, trying to shove his body off mine. I felt like I was suffocating. The more I struggled, the heavier he became. The room spun. I was pinned down like a butterfly on a board, unable to move my arms or legs. Pain throbbed in my head. Jim would be angry if I didn't stop this.

'Daniel,' I begged. 'Please stop! Get off—'

And then I felt it. Like a thousand knives shooting through me, ripping my insides to pieces. Pain like fire. I cried out.

Daniel pushed himself up and looked me in the eyes. 'Theresa, you were telling the truth?'

I looked down between my legs and stared at the blood-soaked sheets, my track shorts around my knees.

Speechless and in shock, I felt sick.

'Wait here,' Daniel said. Moments later I heard water running in the distance and voices speaking foreign words came from other rooms. I thought I could hear several people arguing. I yearned to run away and hide in the comfort of my own warm bed. But I was stuck in a house with no way of getting home. How could I go home, walk in the front door, face my mother or talk to Jim on our nightly phone call? Overwhelmed with shame I chastised myself for being naive, for betraying myself, Jim, my parents, and God. Naked and bloody, my head pounding, I blacked out. I felt Daniel shaking me.

'Theresa.' He shook me again. 'Theresa.' Reluctantly I opened my eyes. Daniel was back. 'Come here with me, Theresa. Be quiet.'

His hand on my elbow, I followed obediently.

'I didn't know,' he said. 'I thought you were just saying that.'

He led me to the bathroom and closed the door. He motioned towards the tub and I stepped in. Sinking into the water, new pain stabbed my privates, jolting me back to reality. I was in a stranger's home. People I didn't know were milling around the house. People who probably didn't know I was there, lying naked in a bath, in front of a young man, feeling as if I was bleeding to death. And I had lost something vitally important. My virginity.

I felt as if I was outside of my body looking down upon myself. I saw a young, naked girl, crying softly, careful to do as she had been instructed and not make a sound. Her body shook as rampant emotions overcame her and the water rose over her body. My emotions were running high: fear of being discovered, shame of what had just occurred and anger at what couldn't be undone. Bright red blood circled the water, floating around my privates. Tears streamed down my face. How would I get home and what would I say to my mother and my boyfriend?

'I am sorry, Theresa. I didn't know. You should have told me.'

I stared at him as tears ran down my face and as the blood pooled in between my legs. 'I did,' I choked out and then cried harder.

'Shh,' he said insistently. 'My family is downstairs. I don't want them to hear. I don't want them to know you are here.'

Fear set in again. Daniel laid my school track jumper on the sink and left the bathroom, closing the door quietly behind him. I heard his voice outside the door. A new wave of fear washed over me. 'No! Leave her alone,' he kept saying.

I shivered. Had someone discovered I was here? I scrambled out of the tub, and doubled over in pain. I hurried and gingerly dried my sore body. Numb and dazed, I changed back into my high school track uniform.

'You will not,' I heard Daniel say. 'She had nothing to do with this.'

What was he talking about?

'Come on, I will take you home,' Daniel said as he entered the bathroom. 'I have to get you out of here without my mother or aunts seeing you.'

There wasn't anyone in the house when I got there a few hours earlier. But time had stopped for me. It stopped hours before, when I was raped.

Daniel snuck me out of the now bustling house and into his car. We were silent while he drove me home. I don't know how he knew where I lived. I'd never told him my address. Unable to look at him, I got out of the car, entered the house, and went straight upstairs to the bathroom. I stripped off my soiled track uniform and threw it in the dirty laundry basket. My head in a fog, I ran a steaming hot bath.

'T? Is that you?' My mum knocked on the bathroom door. 'Are you OK?'

'Yeah, Mum,' I said, unwilling and unable to tell her the truth about what had just happened. 'Had a rough practice and started my period. I'm taking a bath and going to bed.'

It never occurred to me to tell Mum about what happened. To ask her to go to the police with me so that I could file a report for rape. I was ashamed that I had allowed it to happen, that I had been stupid and not listened to the warning bells and gone home when I could. I thought that she would be mad. I had disobeyed her and gone with an Arab boy to his house. And I thought it would be such a disappointment to my parents to know that their only daughter was no longer a virgin. My mum had told me that if I had sex before marriage, the odds were that I would get pregnant and if that happened, she would kick me out. I know now that she was using tough love, trying to scare me into being a good girl. All that matters is that I believed her.

Alone in the tub, I wept over what I was sure would be the worst thing that would ever happen in my life. But that awful afternoon failed to compare with what was to come.

6

A different girl

Pleading sore muscles from track and menstrual cramps, I evaded school for several days. Depression swooped over me like a shadow and I felt separated from my body. I didn't leave my room, didn't accept Jim's phone calls, and couldn't write the daily letters we had exchanged for the past year. How could I act as if nothing had happened? The guilt was suffocating and then the voices started. It had been my fault. I could have prevented it. I should have done something. I shouldn't have gone with him. I berated myself with the same accusations I would later hear from others.

Daniel called my private line several times but I ignored the phone. I was in so much shock that it didn't occur to me to wonder how he'd got my private number. He left messages for me, and his deep, suave, slightly accented voice that had once made my knees wobble now churned my stomach.

When the excuses ran out and I could no longer escape school, I returned a different girl. I got through the morning without seeing Daniel. I didn't go to the school store and he rarely stayed for lunch so I didn't see him in the canteen. He would normally go out with his Chaldean friends for lunch or return home for a hot meal provided by his mother, aunts, or grandmother.

That afternoon, I turned the corner of the hall to go to my locker and stopped dead in my tracks. Leaning against my locker, arms crossed over his chest, was Daniel, waiting for me with a scowl on his face. 'Why haven't you answered my calls? I need to talk to you,' he whispered. 'It's urgent.'

I stared at him. My once feisty spirit had disappeared.

'I'm sorry,' he said.

I wanted to believe his apology but the part of me I had been saving for marriage was gone. He had stolen it and I hated him for that.

'I'm sorry you didn't listen to me,' I replied. 'You should have believed me. You've ruined everything. I have a boyfriend.'

I wanted him to feel bad. Did he want me to tell him that it was OK? That I understood why he hadn't respected me or listened to my wants or needs? In one act, he had ruined my life.

'We need to talk,' he urged. 'Really. There is a problem. I'm sorry.'

He was talking too fast. Mechanically. As if it was a well-rehearsed speech. 'Skip track practice and meet me at my car. It is a matter of life or death.'

I was tired of hearing him apologize. I didn't believe it for a second. Nor did it matter anymore – he had raped me. The bell rang and I turned and ran to class.

In study hall, I sat next to the only other people who might know something that could help me out: the two Chaldean misfit cousins. No longer bubbly, I was somber and sullen. I confided in them, giving them the least amount of information possible. I told them that Daniel had asked to meet me but he had done something terrible to me and I didn't want to meet him. Despite my fear, something inside made me feel as if I needed to go. I felt I had to hear what he had to say.

His cousins told me it wouldn't be a smart choice to stand Daniel up. I didn't understand what they meant but the grave look on their faces told me I should listen to them. On their advice, I decided to meet Daniel. I justified meeting him with the fact that my religion teaches people to forgive. What Daniel had done was between him and God. I would have to battle with it every day, but so would he.

In the parking lot, next to his fancy, expensive car, Daniel stood and held in his hand a white envelope. 'I almost wish you hadn't come,' he said.

'You said it was a life or death situation. Whose?'

'Yours,' he answered.

Fear swept over me.

He continued, 'Something terrible happened the day we were together. I really am sorry about that. If I could take it back, I would.'

'Well, you can't,' I retorted.

'I thought we were the only ones in the house that day, but we weren't. My cousins must have come in the room after we had been there for a while. I am really sorry.'

I couldn't figure it out. If they had come in later, then they had witnessed him raping me. Why was my life in jeopardy?

'Theresa, I don't know how to tell you this, but they saw us together. They took pictures of you.'

Bile rose into my throat. My knees buckled and I grabbed on to the hood of his car for support. Daniel reached to help me. I recoiled. 'Don't touch me!'

'They told me they will give the photos to your dad if you don't do things for them. You have to earn the pictures or they will hang them around the school, church, and show your friends. They are cruel. You must do what they say.'

I remembered the time they had threatened me at school and spat on me.

'I tried talking them out of it,' Daniel continued, 'but they want you. You have to work for them to get the pictures back.'

'What do you mean, Daniel? I don't believe you. Nobody would do that. What do I have to do to earn them back? I don't understand. Like work in your family's store or something? Like do their homework?'

Daniel stood there for a long time. He slowly reached into the envelope and pulled out a picture. He looked at the image and sadly handed it to me. The photo showed my arms on his shoulders, partially clothed bodies intertwined. It appeared to be a romantic union, not the rape that it was.

Tears rolled down my cheeks. How would my father view this? What would it do to his career if the pictures were shown to his boss? What would Jimmy think if he saw this? The priest at church, the youth group I sang in, my brothers, teachers and my friends who knew I had a crush on Daniel: they would believe what they saw. They wouldn't believe my explanation. I had no proof that it had actually been rape.

His cousins knew this. Daniel knew it, too. I looked up at him. 'Now what?'

'They want you to meet them tonight at my house to earn the pictures. You have to have sex with them.

Do whatever they say and then they will give you the pictures. They promised me. I even talked to my older brother, Jonathan. They listen to him but he said he wouldn't do anything. I tried, Theresa. I'm sorry. It's my fault. I told them what really happened and they didn't believe me. I told them you don't do this. You're not that kind of girl. But they don't care. Theresa, if you don't do this, they will hurt your brothers. They know a lot about you and your family. They know where your dad works and that he is away a lot and that you and your brother walk to school.'

I was too stunned to talk.

'Just do what they say and it will be over soon. Then you can go your own way and no one will ever know anything. Please. I will keep trying to talk to them. I will try to help.'

'You've done enough already, Daniel. I just can't do that. I'm not that kind of girl. You know that. I have to think about this, about what I'm going to do.'

'Don't take too long. They are serious, Theresa. I've seen what they have done to others who didn't do what they wanted. I don't want that to happen to you,' he said. 'I like you a lot.'

I turned to walk home, yearning to go somewhere safe where I could hide. I saw my brother Pat walking home. I could tell he was upset. Since our move here, he had seen me upset plenty of times too. Our house, this town, there was something terribly wrong here. Pat and I got along one minute, laughing on our way home from school and then, the moment we entered the house, it felt like a black cloud dropped over us and destroyed the mood. We joked that we lived in a haunted house. We tried to make the best of it, knowing that it probably wouldn't be long until we would move again, but it was taking a toll on our family. At school Pat was being bullied. Sensitive and emotional, he couldn't defend himself well. At home, my brothers and I fought constantly, even my parents fought when my dad was home from his many business trips. Mum questioned his late nights with customers at local bars. Depressed, she shut herself away in her bedroom, drinking heavily and leaving me to care for my brothers.

My mind raced as we walked home from school. I didn't want to shame my family, to add to their burden. The tension at home was building. Surely these men wouldn't make me do anything really bad, I thought to myself. They were bluffing. How I wish they had been.

Patrick slowed down and looked over his shoulder. 'Hey T,' he said. 'There's a car following us. I'm scared.'

An expensive-looking black car with tinted windows followed at a distance. They were letting me know they were there.

'It's OK, Pat,' I said, putting on a brave face. 'Let's cut through the neighbor's yard. I'll race you.'

Later that night, the harsh jangle of the phone jarred me from a deep sleep and I clumsily reached for it near my bed.

'Theresa, I need to see you right now. It's urgent.'

I recognized the voice. It was Daniel. The icy fingers of fear gripped my heart.

'Are you crazy? My parents are here. I'll get in trouble. I'm not allowed out this late. It's after midnight!'

He didn't let me finish. 'This isn't an option. This is it. They want to meet with you right now.'

'When?'

'I'll pick you up right away.'

'Where?'

'Behind your house. On the street before yours.'

'Why?' I was so confused.

'Theresa, I mean it. You have to do this or they'll tell your dad. They are prepared to hurt you if you don't come. I'll meet you in ten minutes.'

In shock, I quietly pulled open my dresser drawer and pulled out a pair of sweat pants and a T-shirt. I put them on and made my bed up to look like I was sleeping in it. I gently opened my bedroom door and crept down the hall at a turtle's pace. I passed my parents' bedroom door that was shut and locked, turned the corner and took each step slowly, one by one. Once downstairs, I walked through the front hall, past the kitchen and through the family room. I unlocked the sliding glass door that led to our backyard and slid it open, inch by inch, until I could squeeze my body out of it. I had never snuck out before. I felt my heart racing. Once outside successfully, I pulled the door shut but kept it open a crack so I could get back inside later. I ran through the heavily landscaped back garden, the water fountain statue and beautiful flowers and bushes, through to the neighbors' garden and out to the street.

Within a half hour, I was back in Daniel's home. The memory of my blood floating in their bathtub came rushing back and I felt sick and terrified at what was to come. This time, Daniel snuck me in through the back door and down the stairs. The steep, richly carpeted stairs led to a door. He opened the door to an elaborately decorated basement. The large living room in there smelled of musk and other foreign scents I couldn't identify. A big-screen TV, huge stereo system, and oversized furniture gave the room a dominating masculine feel.

Also in the room were six impeccably dressed men sitting down in a group smoking, drinking coffee and talking in Arabic. I guessed they were in their twenties. I grew more nervous by the second. They appeared to laugh at me, amused by my presence. Unsure of what to do, I looked at Daniel. As if on cue, his two cousins came around the corner and into the main room. The same two who spat in my face at my locker. A fresh wave of fear washed over me and I reached out to grab Daniel's arm, chiding myself for turning to the person who had started all this mayhem.

'Well, nice to have you here, Theresa,' said one of the cousins.

Yeah, right, nice for you, I thought but was smart enough not to say.

'As Daniel told you, we have some things you want. But there is a condition. You will have to earn them back. And if you don't – not that you have a choice,' he paused, looking at his companions and laughing as he spoke, 'there will be consequences. Are you pre-pared to do that?'

I stared at him. What was I supposed to say?

'Follow me,' the other cousin demanded.

I looked at Daniel.

'Come on, guys,' he pleaded. 'Do you really have to do this? It isn't her fault, come on!'

The short and stocky cousin, Nick, looked at me. 'Do you want the photos or not?'

Daniel and I exchanged looks. He just shrugged. I hung my head and followed his cousin, still not completely understanding exactly what would be demanded of me. We walked through the large room to an area that opened on to two other rooms. Bedrooms, I guessed. One of the doors was closed. Nick led me to the open door. In the large bedroom, gold and burgundy silk fabrics covered a four-poster mahogany bed. It was the largest bed I had ever seen. My parents were well off, but I had never seen money like this. Mirrors were on the walls and the ceiling. This place and the people in it reeked of money, masculinity, and power.

Behind me the door slammed. Daniel's quieter cousin had followed and locked the door, shutting Daniel outside. I was instantly terrified. Why did I want Daniel here, wishing he were protecting me? It made no sense. He was the one who had broken my heart and brought me to this scary situation.

'You will do as I say,' Nick ordered. 'Whatever I say. You want the pictures back? You want to keep your family safe? You want your daddy not to find out that you aren't his little princess anymore? To know you did the dirty little deed? That you're no longer a virgin?'

I thought I would choke on the lump that formed in my throat as he listed my sins. He leaned close, his breath hot on my face. 'You want to keep your sweet little puppy alive? Keep your brothers safe? Make sure nothing happens to your mother and father?'

I nodded meekly.

'Don't even think about telling anyone or not obeying. I will personally deliver the photos to your father at work. Show his boss. Our priest at church. The kids you sing with. Post them on the notice-boards at school for everyone to see.'

The memory of him spitting in my face while the campus policeman pretended not to see assured me he was not bluffing.

'All right, you work for me. Work off the pictures.' He fingered my hair and I cringed. 'With that creamy white skin and blond hair, you will be an asset to my business.' He let my hair drop back into place. 'When you have done as I say, I will give you the pictures. And only then.'

I thought of the humiliation I would feel if the priest and kids at school saw those damning photos. I thought of my new little puppy that my brother had spent his allowance on for me. Mostly, I didn't want my father to learn that I was no longer a virgin. I wanted to protect my mother and brothers while my dad was away traveling. I wanted him to continue working and keep our reputation safe.

I don't remember how I ended up on the bed or naked, but I remember Nick's weight pressing upon me, telling me to be quiet, forcing himself into me. Not only did I endure excruciating pain, but also I was shocked at the brutality of the act. He roughly shoved me around, contorting my body into odd positions. Before I could begin to recover from the assault, the quiet cousin was on me, taking advantage of me for his own selfish pleasure. Tears ran down my face. Little did I know that they were actually being nice to me.

The ruthless pounding against my tender flesh caused my vision to go dark. I was nearing unconsciousness when the torture stopped. I waited a few minutes, afraid to open my eyes just to see that another man waited his turn. Unable to take another moment in the dark, I cautiously opened my eyes. I was alone and naked. I struggled to keep from vomiting, the smell of a mixture of body fluids was rank. Again, tears coursed down my cheeks. The door opened and I cowered. It was Daniel. Entering slowly, he looked at me with pity. He started to say, 'I'm sorry,' but I cut him off.

'Shut up, Daniel,' I hissed. 'This is all your fault.'

Scrambling about, I found my clothes and dressed. Within an hour I was back home, transported in silence by Daniel. In my room, I ran the bath, not caring if anyone heard. I soaked in the tub without interruption. My family slept soundly. Soaking my bruised body, I relived over and over again the horror that I had experienced, trying to soak away the sins of the night, the evil that had claimed my body.

As I reached for a clean towel to dry off, I realized I had walked away without the pictures.

7

A one-girl harem

A few nights later, I was called again. I snuck out and Daniel picked me up in the same location. I had secretly hoped that the first time would be the last but I was very naive.

This time we drove a bit farther out of town and stopped in front of a massive home in a ritzy neighborhood. There were a lot of cars in the driveway, all foreign cars that seemed brand new and top of the line. I followed Daniel into the house via the side door. I entered the front room and instantly felt as if I was on parade as he walked me through the group of hungry-looking olive-skinned men. They lounged around, sitting on richly colored, ten-foot-long couches that were so low it seemed as if they were right on the floor. Large dishes of pistachios and bowls overflowing with fruit shared the coffee tables along-side an abundance of guns and piles of cash. A smoky haze and strong stench of incense from the hookahs permeated the room as haunting Arabic music played loudly. The combination of colors, smells and rhyth-mic beats was mesmerizing and intoxicating, but not in a good way – it was suffocating.

The men ranged in age from those who seemed like teenagers to those in their fifties. Some looked up and laughed, others ribbed the men seated next to them while jeering at me as I walked by. I held my head down, afraid to look anyone in the eye for fear that they would stop me and make me stay with them. Hands reached out and pawed at me, grabbing and pinching, daring me to say something. I had to fight back the urge to snap as I was too afraid of the repercussions of what might happen to me if I did. Deep down inside, my old voice, the one that was strong and opinion-ated, ached to say, 'Hands off, buster' or 'Go to hell!'

I lost count of how many men came into the bedroom that night. When they had finally finished with me, Daniel came into the room and gave me back my clothes and I carefully got dressed as my whole body ached. I was the only white person, the only female, an object to these men. I felt like I was a one-girl harem. I was escorted out of the bedroom and back through the den.

*

As time went on I started to lose my feisty spirit. When I had first moved to Birmingham and had to go back to junior high, even though I had previously just been in high school, I met a nice boy named Tony. He had just broken up with his long-time girlfriend who went to a different school. He had long, dark hair and was very cute in a bad-boy sort of way. He would talk to me a lot outside of school and shared some of his unhappiness and past with his ex with me. She was very jealous and controlling, even physically abusive at times. He was a little mixed up and I took him under my wing and gave him advice as if he were my brother. Nothing ever happened between us sexually and a few months later he got back together with her.

I had spent a lot of time at the pool that summer and his house was close by so sometimes I would ride my bike to see him if I was bored and we would hang out. When we returned to school for tenth grade at the high school, I walked into my science class on the first day and saw Tony sitting at a desk. I was excited to see him, waved to him and smiled. Then I noticed he was holding hands with a very skinny, blond-haired girl. Even though I had never met her, I instantly knew who she was. She stared at me hard but I was nice to her and said hello. Tony was just a good friend but I knew she wasn't right for him and he looked miserably unhappy.

I gave him a questioning look to silently say, 'What's the deal?' and he just shrugged his shoulders in a motion that indicated he had given up. His girlfriend, Becky, had noticed and jabbed him hard in his ribs with her bony elbow. For the months that followed, when I passed her in the school hallway, she would go out of her way to bump into me hard, laugh and walk away. Sometimes my books would drop to the floor. When Tony was not in school, she would throw things at me when no one was looking. She would look at me with a face full of hatred. When she was absent from school one day, I asked Tony about it. He said, 'She hates you, Theresa. She thinks I still like you and she is really jealous.'

I was shocked. 'But we have only been friends, Tony. You shouldn't let someone tell you who you can talk to and be friends with.'

Odd that I was giving someone advice considering what I was silently enduring at nighttime.

He just shrugged and said, 'Be careful of her. She likes to fight.'

I was stunned. I had never fought before. I had been taught to argue your opinion and state your case, fight with words, not fists. I loved speech class – I could take either side of an issue, any issue even if I knew nothing about it, and bring down an opponent using words, expression and facts. It was an exhilarating feeling to win a debate and gave me a sense of power.

But I had never been in a physical fight before. Girls didn't fight. I had heard my dad telling my brothers all my life that boys didn't hurt or hit girls and I hadn't even been in a fight with them.

Becky had a friend who was always around her. She was very unattractive and bossy. She had short brown hair, was tall and gangly, and wore big, unfashionable glasses. One day, near the time of my birthday, the halls were really crowded as everyone changed classes and Becky bumped into me, sending me flying into a locker. Tony wasn't in school that day and her friend stepped in between us and blocked my path so I couldn't walk down the hall and get to class.

'What are you? Her bodyguard?' I said angrily.

I had had enough. I wasn't going to take this a minute longer. I tried to reason with words. 'I don't get it. I haven't done anything to her.' I tried again when I got no response and she still blocked my path.

'You tried to take Tony from her,' the girl replied defiantly.

'No I didn't. We are just friends. We met when they were broken up anyway. He is free to be friends with anyone he wants to be. She doesn't rule him.'

Becky stood in the background not responding to the heated discussion that involved her. But she gave me a look of pure evil. A crowd was starting to gather around us. I thought, this is just crazy.

'If you know what's good for you, you will stay away from Tony.'

The hairs stood up on my neck. I was really mad. No one threatens me, well at least not a girl.

'What if I don't? It's a free country. I can talk to anyone I want!' I stubbornly stood my ground.

I might not have been able to do anything about what was happening to me at night, but I refused to let some bossy girl push me around during the day.

'Then you'll regret it, slut.' She got close to my face and pushed me hard.

I stumbled backwards and my back hit the wall of lockers. There was a huge crowd gathering by now.

My blood was boiling but I didn't want to react. So I just stood there as she continued to push me verbally and physically. 'Come on, hit me,' she taunted.

My hands ached to reach out and hit her but I refused to belittle myself. Then she said it. 'I dare you!'

That's all it took. She had said it. I never turned down a dare. Never. My brothers knew that was the one way to get me to do something.

'You said it,' I responded, as I slapped her across the face with full force.

I released all my indignation for how she and Becky treated Tony in that blow as my hand made contact with her face. Her glasses went flying and she seemed stunned that I had actually done it. She dropped to the floor, searching frantically for her glasses before someone stepped on them. Becky ran up to her to help her find them.

I walked around the two girls, as Becky's friend was no longer blocking my path and walked straight to class with my head held high. I had overheard the lessons my parents had taught my brothers: 'Never be the first to start a fight but always be the last to finish it.' This was the last time, for a very long time, that I would stand up for myself.

It didn't help that after all my planning for my special sixteenth birthday party, Daniel showed up. On the Friday, the day before my birthday, all my friends at school were talking about how excited they were about my party. I tried to be excited too but my nighttime activities were making me so tired and unhappy. It was difficult to even force a smile on my face. As the group of us stood around talking about what music everyone was bringing to play, I saw Daniel walk towards me. He rarely approached me during school. I instantly froze and all my friends got quiet.

'Hey T, I'll see you tomorrow at your party!' he said loudly.

Everyone was in shock and my mouth just about hit the floor. I walked straight to the bathroom and threw up. He would be in my house. He would be near my brothers, my parents, seeing the inside of where I lived. And I couldn't stop him coming. I thought he had forgotten all about my party since things were different now. I thought he would know he was no longer invited. But I knew he was telling me that no matter what I did, I had no way out. Even at my own birthday party.

I was finally going to be sixteen. I had waited forever for this moment. But all day long I felt as if I had a dark cloud hanging over my head. Was he really going to show up? What if he said something to my parents? As my friends arrived and it grew later, I felt relieved – perhaps he wasn't going to come after all. I started to relax and let my guard down. We were all singing along to a popular song when I heard the doorbell. As I walked towards the hallway I saw Daniel walking down the other entrance to the basement. He shot me a brilliant smile as he just sauntered in. The rest of the party was a haze. 'See you soon,' Daniel said, as he left last, smiling at me. Several hours later, as I lay my head down in bed, the phone rang. And I knew he hadn't meant he would see me soon at school. So much for my sweet sixteenth.

*

No matter how miserable I was, one thing I simply couldn't give up was singing in the small folk youth group at church. The leader was a male in his twenties who played the guitar along with another guy about the same age who played drums. There were two singers, myself and a girl I went to school with named Nicole. She was in my grade, was a Chaldean and one of Daniel's cousins. They all seemed to be related to one another. I saw her at church every week during Mass, during practice on Tuesday nights and in the hallways at school. It was odd to be in such close proximity to a female Chaldean. She was shy and kept to herself, saying as little to me as possible. I tried to engage her in casual conversation but she was passionate about her music and would only talk about what we were working on for Mass. 'Theresa, let's practice that again. It's not perfect yet,' she would say over and over again at our weekly practice session. She never looked at me directly and rarely spoke to the other band members but had the voice of an angel.

Shortly before Easter, the group leader suggested we practice outside of the weekly meetings on a particularly difficult holiday piece. 'Theresa, why don't you make arrangements to go over to Nicole's house to practice that this week? Your harmony needs improvement and the timing is off.'

Nicole's face paled. 'My house? I can't. I'm busy all

week working at the store. Why my house? Why can't we meet here?' Nicole complained.

'Because you have a piano at your home and they will be decorating the church for Easter. Work it out between you,' he said. End of conversation.

Nicole clearly wasn't happy when she opened the front door of her enormous house to me. She left the door open and walked straight to the piano in the middle of the front room, completely ignoring me and leaving me to shut the door myself. She opened a small triangular box that housed a metronome, which sat on top of the piano. She put a long metal stick in place and swung it. 'Tick, tick, tick' the metronome sounded as it swung back and forth.

An eerie feeling rushed over my body as I stood in Nicole's living room. I had been there many times before but had never come through the front door. My body was tense and I was terrified that I would run into a familiar male and be recognized. 'Let's get started,' she said curtly.

I decided at that moment to be brave and ask her for some advice. I was exhausted from keeping up the charade and was desperate to find a way out. I had been their slave for only two months, but the nightly excursions to various homes and having an unknown amount of men forced on me was taking a deep toll. I felt as if it had been happening for a lifetime. Perhaps a woman from their culture might understand and be able to help me find a way out.

'Nicole, I need to ask you something. I need your help,' I pleaded.

'I am here to help you with music, Theresa, and that's it. Nothing else. Please don't put me in a bad position. I am sure you understand what I am saying.'

That was it. She knew and wasn't going to help me.

Just then, a Chaldean man in his thirties walked by the room. He stopped and looked in at Nicole and then me and back at her again. We both recognized each other and he said in a booming voice, 'What's going on here, Nicole?'

'Uncle, we are just practicing the songs for Mass. She goes to our church and is in the group and the director is making us. It's just for an hour and then she's leaving.' She spoke quickly and was visibly nervous.

He nodded and walked away.

Nicole and I never spoke about this after that day but as she passed me in the hall at school, she would lock eyes with me and smile softly. No words needed to be exchanged. I think she realized that I wasn't doing this by choice. And perhaps she was thankful that I had respected her wishes that day and protected her from unknown harm.

8

Double life

After long days at school and evenings of homework, I would drop exhausted into bed. Around midnight the phone would ring. I didn't bother to brush my hair, apply make-up or change into clothes. I no longer put street clothing on and just went in my pajamas and was barefoot so I could sneak out quieter and faster. Sometimes I would see the neighbor sitting in a lounge chair watching television late at night. I tried to move when he looked away but I am sure at times he saw me run through his yard.

The car was always the same. The black Trans Am that I had been so impressed with the first time I rode inside it. The driver was always the same: Daniel. He would escort me to the pre-assigned location. Sometimes I would argue with him, yell at him to stop this immediately. I pressured and challenged him to stand up to his cousins and demand the pictures back. But the torture and abuse always came, as he sat meekly doing nothing to help me.

This was the routine several nights a week. I never walked the streets or asked anyone if they 'wanted a good time'. The only thing that changed was where I was delivered. I never knew where I was going, what the address was or even what part of town I was in. Usually the location was a remote neighborhood with large, impressive homes. Each time men I didn't know locked me away in a room for hours. I never knew the names of the blurry faces or the naked bodies that mounted me over and over again. Most never spoke a word to me. They were men of all ages, men with money and always of Arabic descent.

No one asked me why I was there, who I was, how old I was or if they could help me. Nor was I ever a participant in the act. I didn't pretend that I enjoyed it. I didn't dress up in lingerie or high heels. Or beg for their attention so I could service them. And I was never given any money for it. I was a slave. Enslaved to serve whoever had been granted permission to walk through the bedroom door where I lay waiting. I was simply in bondage, trying to earn back the pictures. All the while, Nick and the others were earning huge amounts of money. I was only the end of a business transaction.

The men in charge made sure I couldn't get away. Once I was taken into the various bedrooms in the basements, the door was locked. Sometimes Daniel was permitted to come inside with me, sometimes he was forced to wait outside. The door would open each half hour and a new man would enter. Even if I had been able to escape their hold, get out the door, past all the men and up the stairs used by the families, I had no way home. What was I to do? Walk home barefoot in my pajamas? I didn't even know where I was half the time. Nick's threats still rang in my ears. I couldn't leave until they were finished with me. Most of the time I was in a frightened and confused state and tried to block off in my mind what was happening to me. But occasionally I would hear a voice barking outside the room, giving orders. Giving orders to Nick. I didn't recognize the man's voice, and no one ever spoke to me, but I got the impression that he was the one with the most power, more powerful than Nick even.

On a chilly spring night, several months after having become enslaved, an Arabic mother was angry at being locked out of the basement living area of Daniel's house. These highly decorated areas looked like they were designed as sacred dens for men only.

Perhaps she heard my screams. Did she know what they were doing? The torture and agony I experienced so often inflicted by so many?

Around 3 a.m., after at least six men had had their turn abusing my young body, the woman pounded on the locked basement door while numerous men socialized. She was furious. 'Nick, open this door,' she demanded in heavily accented English with Arabic words scattered in the sentence. 'I will tell your mother. I am tired of this. Daniel, come up here right this minute. I won't permit this any longer. I am going to tell your father.'

The men snickered. Through the locked door, they tried to appease her and convince her she had misunderstood and told her to go away. Her fury and yelling didn't faze them but I was scared. What would happen if she found me there? Would she call the police or my parents? She pounded on the door. Nick turned to Daniel and pointed at me. 'Get her out of here, now!'

'How? We can't take her up the stairs and out that door,' he replied.

Nick looked at the small window at the top of the basement wall. I followed his gaze. It was one of those ugly, small windows with a plastic cone outside to keep away leaves. Like most of those windows, it was half full of grass, leaves, and cobwebs. I was afraid to think of what bugs or little animals were living there, too. The window was about two feet by three feet. How would I fit through? A chair was dragged over and Daniel opened the window. He helped me onto the chair, grabbed my legs and pushed me through the small opening. 'Run quietly around the side of the house, to my car. Hide there and I will meet you when I can,' he told me.

Squeezing out like toothpaste from a tube, trying to ignore what I was touching or what was touching me, I heard the woman pounding on the door and yelling in Arabic. The regular threats against my family, the continuous exploitation and sleep deprivation had brainwashed me, and somehow I was convinced that being discovered by this woman would be worse than what I was experiencing. Only later did it occur to me that she might have been my way out. Being found may have been what I needed to stop the torture.

When I reached Daniel's car, I crouched down low on the gravel driveway near the passenger door, waiting for him. After what seemed like an eternity, he came and took me home. I was shaking uncontrollably due to the fear, exhaustion and physical trauma of the last few months as we silently drove home.

*

I had developed a real problem with my palms sweating profusely when I entered puberty but because of the added stress in my life the sweating now got worse. Every time I got nervous around people, which was almost all the time now, my hands started to drip sweat. I could hold up my hands and see the beads of sweat forming on my fingers and palms and then run down my arms. I didn't like when people touched my hands because I was very embarrassed by it. My mum took me to the doctor for it, who said it was nerves and gave me a special powder to put on my hands when they started to sweat. This only dried up the sweat, it didn't prevent them from sweating, and my hands would become pasty and the white powder ended up all over my clothes. It was very awkward.

Around this time I also started to have a lot of stomachaches and my heart hurt a lot, especially when I was in gym class and ran or was very active. Many times I would have to stop because my chest hurt. My mum was concerned and took me to see a doctor of internal medicine. I imagine she was concerned due to the problems my brother David had had as a baby with his stomach.

I had an upper GI done and they found that I had an ulcer and a large hiatal hernia, which was resulting in a great deal of heartburn. The doctor told her that stress could irritate this but he had no idea the amount of stress I was under. This condition plagued me for many years to come.

That spring, it was impossible to enjoy my favorite season. Though I tried to work hard to get back the photos, it was never enough. The disappointing answer would always be the same. 'Next time.' I was strained to breaking point, trying to maintain friendships with people who knew nothing of my dark secret, pasting a smile on my face at home, running on the track team, hiding my private horror from my long-distance boyfriend and keeping the Chaldeans happy.

In May my mum and I traveled to Cleveland for my first formal dance. Before we left for the dance, we both had to endure a stern lecture from both Jim's parents and my mother about not having sex. They had no idea that Jim and I already had an understanding that we would wait until our wedding night, let alone that I had become a sex slave to men back home. Jim and I went to dinner with his friends and then went to his prom where we danced for a few hours. The boys were focused on partying and drinking and wanted to get to the hotel room they had rented, even though they were underage. Jimmy and I had our turn in the bedroom in the hotel room but remained true to the vow we shared.

We lay in bed together, kissed and talked for a few hours. We talked about what he was going to do when he graduated, what he wanted to do with his life and when we would marry. He was planning to join the

Air Force and would be going away. I was sad about this and needed him close to me. Running away or quitting school to be with him crossed my mind but I knew that would be running from my future too, though there were many times I didn't feel as if I had a future anymore. We talked about the importance of remaining moral and looked forward to consummating our marriage someday as virgins. I cringed inside every time we talked about it and many times that night I wanted to share my torture with him. I wanted to ask him to save me, to take away the pain, to make the nightmare stop.

But I was afraid. I was afraid he would be hurt if he found out what was happening to me. I was afraid I would lose him if he found out I was a long way from being a virgin. I was more frightened of the consequences of revealing the secret than continuing to live it. I kept my mouth shut and suffered in silence. As the days went by, I wondered whether this was happening to other girls too. Was there more to it than lustful, cruel, evil men? Was I a pawn in a far larger, more dangerous game?

I felt like I was a temporary distraction to relieve boredom for some and a luxury item for others – something normally off limits to these men. The more involved I became, the more I realized I was in deeper than I could have even imagined. I started to believe that this deeply connected family 'business' was really a front for an underbelly of evil doings. They were making a lot of money. I belonged to all of them for a price. A price I didn't set or collect. I had no say as to who bought me, for how long or for what act. All of it had been predetermined between my captor, my owner, really, and the men who earned or bid on me.

On those nights when I was raped repeatedly by Chaldean men, I overheard snippets of conversations but not the full essence of them. I heard the name Jonathan uttered over and over again. On an international level, the United States wasn't happy with the Middle Eastern countries. Prices for oil and gas were rising. Inflation was rampant. War seemed imminent. I could feel the tension, even in Detroit, and I was living my own personal war, which didn't feel like it was ever going to end.

9

Summer break

I wasn't called much during the school summer vacation. I heard that Daniel, Nick and his cousin were away for the holidays. Apparently, many Arabic boys and men traveled back to the Middle East to get reacquainted with family members during the summer. They took money home and would return with more family members. Those who stayed here worked full-time in their fathers' grocery or liquor stores. Regardless of the reason for the break, I was grateful for the chance to heal my soul and body.

During this time my family continued to go on regular camping trips in our camper. At first I found it hard being away from the reach of the telephone in my room, as I was terrified that they would come to my home and find me gone or call and I wouldn't be there to answer and there would be repercussions. During these trips I felt free, yet always looked over my shoulder, even while walking to the bathroom in a remote location in the middle of the night with my flashlight. I was still guarded, temperamental and moody but tried my best to lighten up.

We swam during the daytime and at night would walk down to the camp store that was stocked with candy and to the game room full of video machines and pool tables. All the kids hung out there at night and there were always cute boys my age or much older than me. They would flirt incessantly. Perhaps they smelled the sex and experience on me, I thought. Surprisingly, on this occasion I welcomed the male attention I received because it made me feel in control and powerful for a change. And it wasn't tied to having to earn something back. I could be a normal teenage girl where no one knew me. But after letting a boy kiss me one night, and experiencing him ignoring me the next day, I learned that they weren't much different from the other males I had encountered. They valued me just as the others had, as an object.

A modeling agency approached me and invited me to take modeling classes. It was nice to feel beautiful again. My mum went with me to meet with the director of the agency. 'What do you want with my daughter?'

I shrunk in the chair, wishing she would be nice and not ruin this chance for me to do something positive.

'Your daughter has a unique beauty. She holds a great deal of expression in her face and has a beautiful smile. With the right training she could make a lot of money. Money for college.'

'What kind of training?'

'First, we need photos. She'll have a makeover with a professional make-up artist, her hair done, and you could take pictures on your own to save money. Just to see if she looks good for the camera.'

'And after that?'

'It's one hundred dollars for the hair and make-up. If the pictures are good, then she would be signed on for jobs. She needs classes to learn how to move, which would be recouped with the money she makes.'

Mum narrowed her eyes. As my parents were financially stable, things like this were not a priority. Clothing and material items were not of value to them. Family and vacations were more important. But for me it wasn't about the money, I wanted to do this for my self-esteem.

She looked around the room. Not at the glamorous pictures of women on the walls, but at the couch in his office. 'We'll think about it.'

The following week, I had my makeover and

hair done. Mum had agreed and I was so happy. Jim was coming to see me with some of his friends so I scheduled the session for the day of his arrival. The makeover took hours, sitting still while I was painted, my hair rolled and teased and sprayed.

At the end of what seemed like forever, I looked in the mirror. I was beautiful. My mum located several used gowns from friends and the local Goodwill store. Dad proudly took the pictures. My favorite was a gold lamé turtleneck long-sleeved gown that matched the natural gold in my hair. I looked like a slender, sleek model.

Jim arrived that night to see a new me. I was proud of how I looked. After hours of preparation his response crushed me. 'I like you better the way you were,' he said.

I ran to the bathroom and removed pounds of paint. I felt rejected, disappointed that he wasn't happy for me. If he couldn't accept that I was growing up, he would never accept the secret I had carried for the last few months. I would never be able to tell him what was happening. Though he said he loved me, I now felt it was conditional – on how he had seen me in his mind's eye, not how I wanted to look like. I felt like my captors had taken Jim away from me, too. I wanted him to like the changes on the outside, to see me as a woman, and yet he hated that. If he couldn't accept me looking more mature and beautiful, then how could he accept my internal flaws? I could remove the make-up from my face, but I couldn't remove the loss of virginity or impurities from my body.

At that moment, I knew he would never accept me if he knew what I was being forced to do with hundreds of men.

We submitted my modeling pictures to the agency and they called to meet with my mother again. I stood close, listening in as she spoke on the phone. 'Mmm hmm,' she murmured. 'Yes.'

I was hopeful. Without anything good in my life, I wanted this so badly. I needed it, for my sanity.

'I don't think we're interested,' I heard my mother say. 'We move a lot and she couldn't commit to doing it for the long term. Considering the amount of money involved, I don't think it would be advisable,' she concluded and hung up the phone.

I looked at my mum in astonishment. 'Why can't I? The pictures were great.'

'It costs a lot of money,' she explained. 'We'll probably only be here for another year. This is a long-term thing. Besides, guys like that director only want young girls for one thing. You saw that couch in his office. He just wants our money and to have sex with you.'

'But, Mum—'

'And to be honest, you're vain enough already. I

don't want you to get worse. Always primping in front of the mirror. It's for your own good,' she said flatly.

The couch was the last thing I was worried about. I had been enduring endless nights of torture that she didn't know about, and she was worried that this man would want to have sex with me? How comical. How ironic. My chance to have a normal life cut short because she thought a man would want to have sex with me.

That summer we took our pop-up camper, loaded the van, and spent the days sightseeing in Toronto and our nights telling ghost stories around the campfire with my little cousins. Jim had just graduated high school and we weren't able to see each other because he was working full-time and I was away on vacation a lot with my family.

I tried to relax but began to look for a way out. I needed a protector – I couldn't tell Jim so I needed someone else to look out for me, someone older to help me escape. After we came back from our trip I went to the private pool we belonged to with my friends. My body was budding from that of a girl's into a woman's, and I sensed that I had a sort of power over men. Older boys and men sensed my developing sexuality. I liked using the new power to gain control over men, instead of them controlling me. At the pool there were two American guys who were four years older than me. When we were alone, I told them what was happening and that I needed their help. 'You're one of the Chaldeans' girls?' one asked incredulously. That was the last time they spoke to me.

At work, I bonded with a nice young man called Scott who was five years older than me. He hadn't gone to college and had never had a girlfriend, was a bit of a nerd but a good athlete. He had big, fuzzy hair, large glasses, and was aspiring to be a manager at Burger King, although he wished he had pursued his dream of playing professional baseball. I hoped he would protect me and I believed he was probably looking for his first sexual experience. I secretly thought if the Arabs returned home and saw I had a boyfriend, perhaps they would leave me alone when school began.

Scott wasn't my usual type and I really didn't want to be with any guy at all but I was vulnerable and desperately needed help so I agreed to see him outside of work. We started to date. He loved the fact that I was a younger girl and he showered me with gifts and compliments, not knowing anything of my past or connections to the Chaldean group. It felt good to be liked for me. He put me up on a pedestal and, as odd as that felt, I started to trust him. Perhaps he was different from the other men. He was a sweet young man and wouldn't harm anyone. I liked that about him. Maybe he could help me find a way out.

His friends and co-workers partied a lot and liked to smoke pot and drink but I would just sit there and watch them. I didn't want to lose control. I wasn't sure what I would say and needed to keep myself in check. All the while I would be trying not to think about the secret life I would have to return to when summer was over.

As August and the beginning of school drew ever closer, I began to climb back into my shell. One afternoon when I was hanging out with Scott I decided that it was now or never. I tapped into my old bold self and started to confide in him. I was desperate for help, for a knight to save me before the Chaldeans returned. 'Scott, I need to tell you something. I need your help.'

'Sure, baby. What is it? You know I'd do anything for you,' he replied.

I had recently convinced Scott to try out for the Detroit Tigers baseball team. He was very talented and had been recruited right out of high school but had had such low self-esteem that he hadn't gone through with it. He was in a great mood from the prospect of making his dreams finally come true, which had brought about a surge of much-needed confidence.

'You know those Chaldeans that come into the restaurant all the time and stand around? The ones from my school?' I probed.

Sometimes the cousins would stop by my work and stand silent in the doorway. They never ordered anything or came up to talk to me. They simply watched, reminding me that I couldn't escape and I'd better keep quiet. Scott nodded his head.

'Well they pick on me a lot and I need you to talk to them. They have even hurt me. I didn't want to tell you but I don't know what else to do and I need your help,' I pleaded, trying to tell him without telling him. I just couldn't bring myself to tell him anymore than that and risk my family's safety.

Scott sat there shocked for a few moments and then a dark look of anger shadowed his face. Oh good, I thought, he's mad at them for hurting me. He will take care of everything and it will soon be all over.

'What? You're mixed up with *those* guys? Are you crazy, Theresa? I thought I knew you. I loved you! Those guys are bad news. They're dangerous. I have my future to think about. I'm sorry, but I can't help you. You'll have to figure it out on your own without me.'

He turned and walked out of the room and I never talked to him again. We were put on different shifts at work but he soon quit and moved into his own apartment. He had run fast from the danger, abandoning me to endure my relentless nightmare.

I paid an even higher price when the Chaldeans returned and found out somehow about what I had attempted to do. I was in this alone.

It was my nightmare.

My torture to endure until I died or escaped somehow.

And I was only sixteen years old.

10

Back to school

School started before I was ready, but then again, would anyone ever be ready to go back to what was waiting for me?

Summer had been a taste of normal life, with sleep-filled nights, shifts at Burger King and vacations with my family.

When school resumed, so did my life as a sex slave. Once again I was the mouse caught by the cat. A good hard swat from the cat stunned the mouse into temporary unconsciousness. Dazed, the mouse attempted to run away but the cat pounced again. Over and over, until the mouse resigned itself to the game and a long tortuous death.

On the first day of my junior year in high school I cautiously went from class to class. I was happy from the restful summer yet apprehensive about my fate. My grades had fallen at the end of my sophomore year as a result of the physical and emotional trauma I had silently endured. Lack of sleep made it difficult to concentrate. It was crucial I buckled down this year and raise my grades if I wanted to get into college.

After lunch, I went to my Business Math class. Math wasn't my strong suit and I was in the remedial class. I entered the classroom and selected a seat at one of the eight-foot-long tables. Shy at first, and not knowing anyone in the class, I used a coping mechanism I had developed whenever I entered a new situation, which was pretending to read, keeping my head down until I made friends.

Without looking up, I felt him enter the room. Chills went down my spine. Daniel took a seat at the table directly in front of me, arrogantly leant back in his chair, inches from me, and smiled. When I thought it couldn't get any worse, his cousins came into the classroom. Their entrance was loud, letting everyone know they were important. Geeky and timid, the teacher became nervous when he saw them. My face was hot, the heat rising up my neck and into my cheeks.

My trafficker Nick and his sidekick whooped and hollered when they saw me. They spoke in Arabic as they elbowed each other in the ribs and smiled smugly at me. Like Samantha in the television show *Bewitched*, I wanted to twitch my nose and transport myself away from this room. Anywhere but here. How would I survive this? I needed help if I wanted to get through another year.

In September, Jim agreed to come visit me for a few days. I hoped that this might be the perfect timing for my protector to take over at the beginning of the school year. If I could show the Chaldeans that I had someone to protect me, maybe they would back off. I hoped and prayed that I wouldn't have to endure this horror for another year.

Jim borrowed a friend's car and drove the two hours from Ohio to Michigan. We spent a great weekend at my house and went sightseeing in Detroit. My mum took us to Greek town and we walked around the big city, playing on the riverfront. He planned to come to school with me on Monday and leave that evening to get back in time for work. It was a real treat when family members or friends got to attend school with a student and I was very excited to prove to everyone this long-distance boyfriend really did exist.

I still didn't have the courage or heart to tell him what was happening to me. It was a double-edged sword. On the one hand, he would be disappointed, crushed and might break up with me if he found out. The other possibility was that his Italian anger would surface and he would fight the Chaldeans and possibly get hurt. These guys were ruthless. Not only had they backhanded me across the mouth numerous times but I'd seen them in street fights with blood gushing everywhere. I desperately wanted out, but not at the expense of my future husband.

Jim didn't make it through the day at my school. He sat next to me in my morning classes and walked with me to my locker. With Jim by my side, handsome and deeply muscled, I couldn't help giving the evil cousins a semi-smug look as I passed them in the hall. But during science class, Jim said he needed to go to the bathroom. He got a hall pass from the teacher and I told him where to find it. He was gone a long time and when he returned, he was different. Now he was quiet, not his usual smiling, fun-natured self.

'I'm going back to the house,' he said after the bell rang.

'Are you feeling OK?' I asked him, concerned.

'Fine.'

'But—' I started.

He bolted through the school doors, abandoning me to face the Chaldeans during math class, alone. At lunch, my friends asked where Jim was. I told everyone that he had suddenly felt sick and had to leave. I left the lunchroom to walk down the hall, trying not to make eye contact with Nick. As we passed, he gave me a snide look and said something in Arabic. I wondered if he had something to do with Jim's quick exit.

For the rest of the day, I felt more alone than ever before. I had been hopeful that it was finally over. I thought Jim would be my protector and save me from further abuse. I thought I could make this happen without having to tell him what was happening to me, that the Chaldeans would see him and leave me alone.

I was naive, unaware of how much I was benefiting others through my body and my pain. They would not let me walk away. They were making too much money from me. After school when I went home I found that Jim was gone. He had gone back to Ohio. No note, no explanation, no goodbye. What did he know? What had he seen or heard to make him leave so abruptly?

A few weeks after Jim walked out on me he called and we had a long conversation but didn't mention what had happened that day at school. From then on we carried on with our relationship but it wasn't as intense as before. I was too scared to ask him why he had fled and he didn't bring it up either so I thought everything was OK. A few days after our talk I was walking home from school along the sidewalk next to a busy road when a car honked at me. My brother Pat had stayed after school for a Christian group meeting. I was used to this and occasionally walked home alone when he was busy. Sometimes a person would blow their horn or a man would dog-whistle at me. I hated the attention. This never happened in the rural areas where I had previously lived. I soon learned that men frequently honked at females and it was common in an upbeat, fast-paced city. When I complained about it to my mum, she viewed the acknowledgments as compliments. She told me to wave back and say thanks. But I didn't want to acknowledge them. The less attention I brought to myself, the better. I certainly didn't need any more of it. The physical and sexual attraction was not wanted. Every time I heard a car horn, I wanted to hide under a rock.

On this day, I sensed that a car had been following me for about a half mile. Being constantly on guard was exhausting. Cars were sometimes parked outside my home watching our movements. The expensive car stopped beside me and the driver's tinted window rolled down. The Chaldean's face was vaguely familiar. He was in his early twenties, not handsome, dressed in expensive clothes wearing plenty of gold jewelry.

A flashback jolted through me. He was one of the many men who had forced himself on me and had been exceptionally brutal. I began to tremble. 'Get in,' he demanded.

'Where's Daniel? I didn't hear I was supposed to go anywhere,' I stammered.

'Get in now.' He pointed to the seat next to him. A large, sharp knife lay on the passenger seat. I looked at him, then at the knife, and then straight ahead. My house was only a half mile away. Was anyone watching? Would anyone see me getting in his car? Could I take a chance and risk running home?

He picked up the knife and pointed it at me. Imagining the sharpness of the blade slicing across my skin, I walked around the back of the car, opened the door and sat down in the passenger seat. It felt all wrong. It wasn't like all the other times when Daniel was with me. Although Daniel was no angel I always felt like he wasn't as bad as the others and would try and help me when he could.

As we drove off, he rested the knife on my leg. I wanted to open the car door and jump out, but sat frozen. I realized I could handle any sex act, but I was afraid of being stabbed. That realization was like cold water being flung in my face. He drove me to a remote area, and pulled the car into a vacant parking lot. Then his hands were on me, tearing at my clothes. I fought him. Suddenly the knife was at my throat.

'I'm tired of sharing you, waiting my turn, earning my time,' he growled. Cruelly he forced my body to his will. 'I wanted you all for myself,' he said afterwards.

The knife lay between us as he drove me back to my house. He opened the door for me to get out. Broken in spirit, feeling alone and helpless, I got home just as my brother Pat walked through the door. It looked natural to my mother for the two of us to come home at the same time. I climbed the stairs and headed straight to the bathroom where I ran the water and soaked in a long, hot bath and cried uncontrollably.

Thankfully the cousins were not in math class the following day. They rarely came anyway. On the days they did appear, there was a marked difference in the way the teacher taught. A timid and reserved man, he ignored the callous remarks by the cousins in their native language but they were still disruptive and loud throughout the entire class making teaching and learning impossible. When the teacher started to reproach them for their behavior, they would stare hard at him without looking away – a look that dared him to stand up to them. He never did.

With thoughts of the day before still fresh in my mind and Daniel sitting inches from me, all I saw were jumbled numbers on the board. A tightly folded piece of paper landed in front of me on my open book. I slowly unfolded the paper. The chicken scratch read, 'They want to see you tonight.' My stomach lurched.

That night I arrived, plagued with memories of the rape by the unknown Chaldean man the day before.

I knew they would find out. They knew everything that happened in my life. Would there be repercussions? Would I have to pay another price for what had happened? I was scared.

In the downstairs living area of Daniel's house, Nick approached me. He rarely spoke to me and I shrunk back in fear, keeping my eyes to the floor. 'I have a question. It is important that you answer correctly, for your own good. Do you understand?'

I nodded, a lump in my throat. 'Were you with another Chaldean this week?' he asked.

Should I lie? Would I get out of there alive? 'Yes. He told me you said it was OK. I thought he was taking me to you. Afterwards, he said he lied and wanted me all for himself.'

Nick turned and left the room. I was terrified that I was going to be punished. The others in the room went about their business, soon forgetting I was there. I overheard his voice in the other room, barking orders and yelling. I don't know what happened but I didn't have to have sex with any men that night and Daniel took me home early. I didn't see the unknown man again for a very long time.

Later on, alone in my bedroom, I wouldn't allow my thoughts to settle on Daniel. Similar to a child with an abusive parent, I had intensely confusing feelings for him. For the first six months I had known him, I had developed a crush on him. He was so charming back then. But now I was angry that he had started all of this. I was angry that he didn't protect me and angry that he wouldn't help me put an end to the horror. But if I allowed myself a split second of truth, I also knew a part of me loved him. Silently he drove me to each den of sin. Though he never did anything to stop the abuse, he never abandoned me. He was always there every time I was assaulted. There in the room, he watched. Sometimes he took care of me if I was hurt badly. Then he would drive me home and tell me how sorry he was. Not being able to take it out on anyone else I would yell at him, 'Then why didn't you stand up to them?' But I never received an answer.

Many years later, when I was attending a Human Trafficking conference, someone said, 'After he raped you, did you ever have sex with Daniel again?'

'No,' I replied.

But as I traveled home from the conference that day, a long-buried memory came rushing back. I allowed it to enter, wanting to know. Ready to handle it. Or so I believed.

There was one other time.

In the winter of my junior year of high school, almost a year after the time my trafficking began, Daniel picked me up after school. His happy mood surprised me. Usually he appeared as sad as I was when he drove me to a house where strange men waited for me.

'I have a surprise for you, Theresa.'

He dropped his voice and mumbled that he wanted to make up for it all. Do something nice for me.

I was confused. A large part of me didn't want to be in this car, didn't want to be with him going anywhere if I didn't have to. I just wanted to go home and sleep. 'Where are we going?' I asked.

'My cousin is letting me use his house while he is at work.' Daniel smiled.

His strange behavior made me suspicious. Soon, we entered a simple, two-story condominium that I had never seen before. As he led me upstairs, my stomach was in knots. Yes, I cared for him, but sex had taken on a totally different meaning for me – especially with Chaldeans. I now believed sex was a way for people to get what they wanted. For me, sex was no longer attached to love and emotions. At sixteen years old, after having sex more times than I could count, I had never had sex with someone I truly cared about. For me, terror was the only emotion that accompanied the act. I didn't know what to do. Did I even have a choice here?

I followed Daniel up the stairs and was relieved that there were no other people in the home. That was a first. Why had he brought me here?

'Theresa, sit on the bed and I will run a bath for you. I want you to relax. I want you to be happy. I am truly sorry for all that has happened to you. It's my fault. I care about you. I always have. I've seen what you have gone through and I just want to be with you. I want you to be my girlfriend.' His voice dropped to a whisper. 'But you know that can never happen.'

Nervously, I sat on the edge of the king-sized bed. The sound of running water caused a flood of memories. The first time, blood all around me.

Trying to take my mind off the fact that I would have to get naked and climb in the bath, I glanced around the room. It didn't look like a Chaldean home. It looked American, with simple furnishings and neutral colors. 'I will give you privacy, Theresa,' Daniel said, coming back into the room. 'Enjoy the big tub. There is a surprise in there, a razor and cream. Shave yourself totally clean, for me.'

Once again, I was instructed to do something; something that would no doubt lead to sex. In spite of everything that had happened to me, back then I still believed all people were good. I didn't want to stop believing that, even though it was a belief that I did not benefit from. I went ahead and started to undress but feelings of betrayal swept over me. How dare he tell me what to do and want to have sex with me? And yet another part of me longed to be in his arms, to feel him protect me rather than abuse me. I was so conflicted.

I was nervous during the bath. I didn't enjoy it. I did as he'd told me and shaved myself clean. But I didn't feel clean. I felt degraded. The whole situation felt wrong. I let the water drain from the tub and wrapped a soft towel around my body. I wanted to go home. Daniel wasn't in the master bedroom when I walked through to it but a green negligee was laid upon the bed. I stared at it, shocked.

'I'm downstairs getting some water to drink,' Daniel called up. 'I left you a little present to make you feel good. You will look beautiful in it!'

I wanted to run back in the bathroom, lock the door, and throw up. Was this a trap? Were other men coming soon? I was nervous because I didn't know if I wanted to have sex with Daniel. I didn't know how to do it with someone I cared about. And I was shocked that he wanted me. He said he loved me, didn't he?

I did as I was instructed and put on the nightgown. Dressed in the beautiful silk and lace, I sat on the edge of the bed. Daniel returned to the room wearing just his trousers. He looked comfortable and happy. He stared at me. 'Wow. You look even more beautiful than I ever imagined,' he said.

My heart was in my stomach. That was the first compliment I had received in a long time. It completely confused me. I was torn between feeling proud and wonderful while at the same time untrusting and damaged. 'I want to take a picture,' he said. 'To always remember you like this. For me. You are mine!'

My heart was happy that he seemed to care for me. That he'd bought me this nightgown. That he wanted me. But he was doing the same thing his cousins had. Take my picture like this? Would he threaten to show it to others too? Suddenly the facts fell into place. He was the same as they were. No different. What would happen if I refused? I had tried that before and always been severely punished. But he said he loved me. Maybe he wouldn't hurt me. Then reality hit me full force. Daniel had been involved in it all along. If I refused to do as he said, then he wouldn't be my protector any longer. I would be out there all alone with people who seemed like the cruelest men alive. I didn't want to take that chance. It was just sex after all. I could do this.

So that afternoon we had sex. Daniel was happy. He was caring and loving, not mean or harsh. But it didn't matter. Like always, I left my body and shut down my heart. Afterwards, he drove me home, as usual. This time he had a smile on his face. He even held my hand. I pretended. I was good at pretending. I felt sick to my stomach, though. I was so conflicted. I silently prayed for this to never happen again.

That night, as I soaked in my bathtub at home as I always did after a man had entered me, I thought long and hard. Tears streamed down my cheeks. These were different tears, tears of betrayal and confusion. Was Daniel in love with me, was he too a pawn in this scheme? Or had he set me up and been fully involved from the beginning? My heart ached. Had they put him up to this? Did he truly love me? Did he feel terrible about what was happening to me, or was he behind this whole thing?

Daniel had done what the others had not been able to do; he had enslaved not only my body, but my heart as well.

11

Always watching

One cold winter morning my mum told me she had a meeting for the international exchange program. She was excited, glad to have something to do that was constructive, creative, and helpful to others. Her schedule included meetings several days each week, rehearsals for plays in the evenings, attending the Gourmet Club several times per month, and entertaining my dad's customers to help him close deals when he was in town. 'Theresa, you're in charge of dinner tonight,' she said. Her busy calendar often resulted in additional responsibilities for me. 'I won't get back until late and your dad won't be back until the end of the week.'

Normally I wouldn't have a problem with this; it was my duty as the oldest after all. But I was so exhausted from the late nights I was subjected to while everyone slept, as well as trying to stay awake during school, that one more chore to do seemed monumental and overwhelming to me.

Thankfully school was uneventful that day and I hoped to get through it without incident. I went to honors English, the only class I was successful at, then later tried to focus on raising my falling grades in my other classes. It was difficult to concentrate when I was constantly wondering what would happen next. When will the phone ring again, where will they take me next, when will the next note appear demanding the use of my body? So far they had only demanded I go at nighttime but Daniel had already warned me that this might change. 'They are very happy with you and things might start to change. I just want to prepare you.'

'What do you mean, Daniel?'

'You want the pictures back, don't you?' he responded and I just looked away.

My last class of the day was study hall where we did our homework. I sat with my Chaldean friends, the misfit cousins from speech class. They tutored me in their language and I helped them write their speeches and English papers. The other students at my school noticed how I helped them out. I knew they also watched me when the evil cousins were confronting me and people saw when I would leave school in Daniel's car. White kids never interacted with the Arab kids. I was the first to have broken into this sacred circle, even though they had no idea I was being forced into it with no way of escaping. They called me Chaldean Lover and Camel Jockey Lover. Even my girlfriends believed I was obsessed with Arab boys. Smiling, I cringed deep inside each time it was said. It was even written in my high school year-book. But I needed them to believe that this was all it was so I never corrected them. I could never reveal the truth of what was happening to me. So I went along with the charade.

I was busy writing an English paper for these misfit cousins when Bassim poked me in the arm. I turned to him with a confused look on my face. 'Look at the door,' he said.

There stood Daniel. What was he doing here? He was usually gone by now, at home or working at his family's store. Dread washed over me. Bassim and Hassam looked at me with sad eyes. 'Bye,' they said knowingly.

I gathered my books and gave the study hall monitor the excuse that I needed to get to track practice early. Silently, I followed Daniel to the car. He held the door open for me, though he was anything but a gentleman, I thought sarcastically.

As always I didn't know where we were going. Today we arrived at his house. The driveway was filled with cars. I shut my eyes as I felt the growing feeling of doom. Servicing men in the daytime felt different to me. I was worried at being found out this way, though I should have welcomed that as a possible way to finally escape my hell. Downstairs, Daniel led me to the bedroom where Nick was waiting. The second bedroom door was open, which was unusual. It was always closed. I tried to peek in to get a glimpse of the man I'd heard so much about, Jonathan. He seemed to be the one in charge. Sometimes I'd heard him outside the room barking orders at the other men who seemed to either revere or fear him.

I was curious about the unseen man who never partook in what Nick was offering to all the men: me. 'Who is that?' I asked Nick.

He stopped suddenly, whipped around towards me and slapped me across the face. 'Never mention him again,' I was told as I rubbed my stinging cheek. 'He doesn't exist. For your own good, don't ever say his name. Understood?'

I nodded my head sadly. I was then instructed to follow him and the other cousin into the bedroom. I was terrified of Nick, who had grown more and more ruthless in his treatment of me. Daniel had tried to step in a few times, telling him to stop before I was hurt too badly. But they never paid any attention to him or his pleas.

'Strip and lay down,' Nick roughly ordered. 'I have something special planned for you today.' I obeyed. Several other Arab men walked into the room as Nick shoved Daniel out the door. 'You can't watch today,' he told him.

'But—' Daniel began to protest.

'Out!' Nick snapped.

Before the door closed, Daniel locked eyes with me and I saw his terror.

'You can't save her today, little cousin,' Nick said as he slammed shut the door and locked it.

This had never happened before, I panicked. I was terrified of what might lie in store for me, things out of my control, with no one to help me survive. I braced myself for the worst as a thought entered my mind: I need to get home and make dinner for my brothers.

Nick started to pull several pieces of rope from the drawer of a large dresser. I'd had a bad feeling about today from the start and I nervously shivered as I watched him. Nick spoke in Arabic to the four other Chaldean men in the room. I understood a little, but not nearly enough. My Arabic lessons had only covered vulgar words and names of food and barely any of it helped in this situation. Was it better to know my fate ahead of time, or be oblivious of the horror to come?

The other cousin grabbed my leg and jerked it to the far corner of the bed. I instinctively jerked my leg back and was instantly sorry for it. Nick twisted my ankle until I felt it would snap in two. I screamed in pain and someone began pounding on the door. Daniel? Nick ignored the door and tied my ankle to the bedpost. Then he tied my other leg to the opposite post. My twisted ankle swelled and my legs lost all sensation. I laid there, spread-eagled, humiliated at being crudely exposed. Tears of shame sprang to my eyes.

Smiling evilly, Nick grabbed my wrists. I whimpered and he laughed as he tied my arms to opposite bedposts. One by one, the men in the room mounted and abused me. They carried on conversations in their native tongue while they were on top of me, oblivious to my pain and horror. I closed my eyes, but couldn't block out their voices, the smell of their bodies, the sound of their grunts and heavy breathing next to my ear. How I desperately longed to be untied from this position that my body was forced into. All I wanted was for Daniel to come and get me and return me home where my brothers were waiting for me.

When the motion, the pounding and the jerking,

ended, I anticipated getting released. I opened my eyes to Nick's sinister grin, looming over me. 'We're not done yet, *habibi*.' He was calling me the Arabic word for sweetheart. It was cruelly ironic. 'You thought that was it?' Hope deflated at the sound of his words. 'I told you I have a special surprise for you. These men,' he looked at the faces around me and they chuckled, 'paid a dear price to be here today. You should feel honored.'

Nick brought a collection of items to the bed, including a large, shiny green cucumber and a bottle of wine. The men had been drinking it while they were in the room and it was now empty. The strange men were laughing as Nick held the cucumber. 'My mother thought I wanted this to eat.' He laughed. 'She doesn't know the other pleasures this vegetable can hold!'

He proceeded to shove the cucumber deep inside of me until I screamed with pain. At that moment I didn't care if he got mad at me for speaking out because the humiliation and shock at the invasion gave me the courage to beg him to stop. 'Please, please stop.'

'Shut up. I don't want the women upstairs to hear you.'

I continued to scream in agony. I pleaded and begged the men to stop. It only seemed to make Nick more determined to exacerbate my pain. In Arabic he instructed one of the men to clamp his hand over my mouth as they continued abusing me. The large, heavy hand over my mouth muffled my screams and nearly suffocated me. From the pain, fear, and lack of air, I hyperventilated. From somewhere very far away, I heard pounding on the bedroom door. The agony seemed to last for hours. Lack of circulation had caused my legs to go numb while the rest of my body burned with pain. I was in shock from the abuse. Finally, mercifully, I lost consciousness.

When I awoke, I was naked on the bed and cut free from the ropes. Seeing a man sitting next to me, I jumped. It was Daniel and he was holding my hand. I tried to move but was too bruised and the pain was too fierce. Eventually, when I mustered enough strength, I got up to leave the bedroom and a deep, older voice boomed from down the hall. The outer room where the men were gathered suddenly went quiet as they realized I was being summoned to him. 'Daniel, bring her in here.' It was Jonathan.

I looked at Daniel and shook my head. I couldn't stand one more man having his way with me today.

'Now!' Jonathan boomed.

Ignoring my objections, Daniel took my hand and gently pushed me into the room. It was lavishly decorated with huge wooden furniture and expensive-looking, richly colored materials. It resembled my idea of what a harem would look like, with luxurious, sheer hanging fabric. Before me, lounging comfortably upon his massive bed, was a stunning Chaldean man in his late twenties. He was the most beautiful man I had ever seen and was dressed impeccably. He slowly looked me over, approvingly. 'Leave, Daniel,' he said. 'We won't be long.'

With my eyes I begged Daniel not to leave but he obeyed his older brother, turned and abandoned me once again.

'Theresa, do you know who I am?' Jonathan said.

I was surprised that he knew my name. But I knew he was the one in charge, the one engineering this from behind the scenes. He was the one profiting from my exploitation.

'Jonathan?' I answered tentatively.

'I can make your life very easy or very hard. Do you know that?'

'How much harder can it be?' I asked sarcastically.

'I know. They treated you very hard today, didn't they?'

I looked at him and nodded. Tears filled my eyes.

'I can take all that away. I can give you a very nice life. I can stop all the pain. Would you like that?' I didn't know what to say. 'Let me put this simply. Either they will continue to hurt you and I will give them permission to do whatever they want to you. Or you can work for me. You have been a good addition to my cousin's business, which in the long run benefits me as well. But I have decided that I want you to be my private charge. I will take care of you and protect you. But, if you don't agree, I can't promise what will happen. Do you understand this?'

I nodded, though I didn't know what he was talking about.

'Think about it. Don't talk to anyone about it. This is between us. Tell Daniel when you are ready to contact me.'

And then I was dismissed.

As always, Daniel drove me home in silence. He stopped at the usual place behind my house. As I reached for the door handle, I looked back at him. 'Did they give you the pictures?' I asked. He looked down and slowly shook his head. 'No.'

I snuck through the neighbor's yard and went into my house. After washing my face, I took the dinner out of the refrigerator that my mother had prepared earlier. Zombie-like, I put the dish in the oven. 'Patrick,' I called to my brother, 'make a salad. I'll be upstairs until dinner is done cooking.'

In my bathroom, tears poured down my face as the bath water poured from the faucet. Crying hysterically, I climbed into the tub. Every part of my body hurt, every organ was bruised. And my soul was crushed.

*

It didn't take long to realize that I was at the Chaldeans' mercy no matter where I was, what time it was or what I was doing. I knew I was watched a lot but I had no idea to what extent. I was soon to find out.

I enjoyed babysitting and made pocket money by taking care of little kids. It came naturally to me being the oldest with three little brothers. Getting away from home, eating snacks and fizzy drinks that my mum would never buy, was nice, but the best part was being out of the dreariness of our house, escaping my responsibilities, the fighting and most importantly – the phone.

After the torturous afternoon with the cousins and the conversation with Jonathan, they mercifully left me alone for a few days. At the weekend I had a babysitting job for a family I hadn't babysat for before. I liked the fact that they lived in the country far from my suburban house. I felt safe as I put the kids to bed and settled down with a fizzy drink to watch a movie. We didn't have cable or movie channels at my house. I relaxed, thinking this was the easiest way anybody ever earned money.

When I heard the phone ring in the other room, I got up to answer it. 'Miller residence,' I said.

'Theresa, what are you doing?'

I couldn't believe it. They were playing tricks on me. Perhaps I had fallen asleep in the chair and was having a nightmare. 'How did you know where I was? How did you get this number?'

This was the second time they had found out the telephone number of where I was – first with my private line and now with the parents I was babysitting for. I never found out how Daniel and the Chaldeans got these numbers, or how they knew where I would be at all times. But it added another level to my imprisonment. I felt like they had people who were watching me and reporting back to them. I didn't know who I could trust anymore. Suddenly a thought popped into my head.

Oh my goodness! Was he outside? I couldn't leave. I would be in so much trouble. I couldn't get out of this one. There were little kids here. I had to protect them.

'We know where you are at all times, Theresa.'

I began to shake. 'What do you want? I can't leave here, no matter what!'

'Don't worry. They don't need you. Not right now, anyway. They just told me to call you and make sure you knew they are watching you. Be careful, Theresa. Jonathan is involved now. They know that and they aren't going to want to lose you so easily. It changes everything.'

'How did you get this number?' I heard voices in the background and something that sounded like the phone had been yanked from Daniel's hands. The line went dead.

The Millers returned home an hour later. I was shaking as Mr. Miller drove me home. 'Are you all right?' he asked.

'I think I'm getting sick,' I replied.

I watched to see if we were followed. At home, I checked in with my parents, telling them everything went well and that I was going to take a bath. Running the bath water, I trembled, realizing that even my private time, my few escapes from the area, were being monitored. I wanted to disappear from the face of the earth. They probably knew I was in the bathtub right at that moment. They knew when my father was out of town. They knew everything. I could be found anytime, anywhere. I was never safe. And my family wasn't safe either. Tears of desperation flowed down my cheeks. How much more would I have to endure? How much longer would I have to pay the price? What was the cost of getting the pictures back, of keeping my family safe and of staying alive?

Several weeks later, I had another babysitting job and they decided to make their threats come true. I was taking care of two little kids in our neighborhood while their parents went to a party. It was close to my house so I had walked there. We had played a game and I fed them dinner and put them to bed early. I was

just starting to relax when the phone rang. Not thinking anything of it, I answered it. 'Theresa? I need you
to come right now. It's imperative. I have some very
special men who would like to meet you.'

But it wasn't Daniel. It was the voice I rarely heard:
it was Jonathan himself. I froze. This was serious. He
had never called me before.

'Umm. I am sorry but I can't. I am busy.' I stumbled
over my words. Did he even know what babysitting
was?

'Theresa, you don't seem to understand, this isn't a
request. It is a *demand*,' he replied.

'I understand but I am not home. I don't know
what to do,' I pleaded.

He obviously knew I wasn't home. He had called
me at a neighbors' house. How had he gotten the
phone number? How did he know where I was going
to be?

'This is what you're going to do. Listen to me very
closely. You are going to leave there in half an hour
and meet Daniel at the regular place. Do you understand me? Am I being clear?'

'OK,' I said into the dead phone.

What was I going to do? I decided that not going
was not really an option. Jonathan wasn't a person to
mess with and I didn't want to have to think about
what would happen to me or my family if I refused

or didn't show up. I called my house and my brother answered the phone. 'Pat. Thank goodness. I need your help.'

'Yeah, what's up?' he replied.

'Can you come over to the house that I am babysitting at that's down the street? It's those two little kids. I need you to take over for me. Please?'

'What? Are you crazy? You can't do that!'

'I have to. Please don't tell Mum and Dad. Just tell them you are coming to help me out and we are babysitting together. I need you to cover for me.'

'I'm not sure, T.'

'I will give you all the money I was going to make tonight if you do it for me,' I offered.

'OK. I'll do it.'

I waited for him to get to the house and showed him around quickly then walked over to the pick-up point in the dark. Daniel arrived in his car and took me to meet the men Jonathan had arranged for me. I was taken to an exclusive penthouse in downtown Detroit. Daniel pulled the car up to a private gate and punched in a code to open it. As he parked the car in a secluded spot, he handed me some clothes. 'Here. He wants you to wear these. They're nicer than what you have on.'

I had been wearing jeans and a sweatshirt. I could tell by the feel of the material that the short skirt and glittery top were of the highest quality. I changed in the car while Daniel watched and then he led me into the elevator where he pushed the button for the top floor. That night I didn't see Jonathan at all but was met by several older, very rich men. One of the men, who seemed to be the host, paraded me in front of the other men, turning me around for their examination and approval while they talked in their language. I was instructed to sit and they offered me drinks and food, which I declined. They talked to one another and ignored me for most of the night while I sat on the couch, and Daniel sat in a chair by the front door waiting.

I didn't have sex with anyone that night but felt just as used. Like a piece of property. I wasn't smart enough to realize that they were examining the property before purchasing it.

Miraculously, I arrived at home around the time Patrick did. Our parents asked how everything went and we lied and told them it was great. Pat followed me to my room and we shut the door. 'Boy, are you in trouble. Those parents were so mad when they came home and saw me there instead of you!'

'Oh no. What did you say?' What would I do if they told my parents?

'Don't worry, T. I told them that you got sick and asked me to cover for you. They bought it. And thanks for the forty dollars! They sure pay good!' he said over his shoulder as he walked out of the room.

To the men who used me night after night, I was not a human being. They performed on me the most intimate act a man and a woman can engage in, but to them I was only a dollar value. To know that this was all I was worth in my formative teenage years, during the period when a woman defines her value and identity, proved devastating. How does a child begin to process this? To know so many, many men didn't care about me at all. That they celebrated my humiliation, degradation and pain. It was a critical wound to my soul. It was a bitter view of inhumanity to an idealistic teenager.

This awareness leads a victims of human trafficking to lose all love, even for themselves. When others don't value or love you, it becomes difficult, if not impossible, to love yourself. Shame, embarrassment, and guilt fill the vacuum where love should thrive. Often the heart and the brain give conflicting messages. My heart was wounded from so many men treating me without care or value. Certain locations, smells, words and songs can trigger memories.

One day a few years ago, a friend and I watched a movie on trafficking called *Call and Response*. As I sat in my theater seat, trying to be strong and not remember what had happened to me, the passionate words of a song penetrated my carefully constructed shell. 'They don't know my name ...'

The memory rushed forward like a wave crashing upon a rocky beach. It was a night when the room I was in smelled of sex, smoke and musky incense. An old, attractive, olive-skinned man entered. He looked upon me, splayed naked on the bed, my hair rumpled, my young body wet and exhausted from being mounted by so many men. Rarely did anyone look me in the eyes but this man did and I saw admiration and sadness on his face. 'What is your name?' he asked in a rough accent.

Knowing I would be punished, I didn't dare say a word. The kind-eyed man seemed out of place among these other brutes. He turned to Nick. 'What is her name?'

Nick looked at him with disgust. 'What does it matter? She has no name.'

His words struck my heart. I turned my head to the side as tears rolled down my cheeks. 'Never mind,' I heard the man say. 'I have changed my mind. The deal is off.'

I turned to watch the dignified man walk out of the room.

I felt Nick's anger. 'Get up and get dressed,' he spat. 'You're no good to me anymore tonight. Get out of here. I will tell Daniel to take you home now. And this better not ever happen again! You are costing me money!'

While I was grateful that I didn't have to endure anything else that night, all I could think of was that this kind man hadn't helped me escape. He hadn't asked me how old I was or if I had wanted to be there. He hadn't asked where I was from, if I could leave voluntarily or why I was doing this. I was worth nothing. I didn't matter. I had no name.

That spring, as I entered my second year of being trafficked, the stress of being constantly watched in addition to the brutal assaults on my young body produced intense trauma. Noticing my grades dropping even further and a difference in my personality, my parents arranged for counseling. The therapist asked what was wrong but I said I was fine. They put my change in temperament down to teenage hormones, having difficulty adjusting to the new home and missing my long-distance boyfriend Jim. Never could they have fathomed what the real reason was.

Week after week, I sat silent during the sessions. The woman talked about boys and all the typical stressors teenagers face. She had no idea about the men and stressors that I dealt with on a daily basis. I rolled my eyes and stared out the office window. After a while, she accepted my silence and gave me weekly lectures. Talking into the air, she discussed issues of self-esteem and valuing oneself. Though I wouldn't admit it at the time, I did listen. She made me yearn for good times to return to my life. I was weary of sneaking out at night, scared of getting caught and more scared of the punishment I would receive if I didn't leave the house. I was exhausted from leading a double life, depleted from being tortured and used over and over again.

After about a month of counseling there was one night when I felt stronger and determined to change my destiny when I was called in to service. I decided that it was time. I wanted the pictures. I deserved the pictures. I had done enough to earn them back. I never knew what each night was going to bring, but things were always worse than I was able to imagine. On this occasion after Nick and several other men had been sexually satisfied and before I lost my nerve I decided to ask. I stood in the room, naked, as Nick dressed. The other men were leaving the room, totally disregarding my presence. 'Nick, can I have the pictures now? I've done more than enough to earn them.' I spoke shyly.

Not looking up, he remained silent.

'I think I have the right to them now,' I pleaded.

All motion in the room stopped. The others stood

in shocked silence. Nick slowly turned toward me, his facial expression reminding me that he was the most evil person I had ever encountered. 'You have no rights here,' he growled. 'I own you and you will do as I say.'

He gripped the gold metal buckle of his belt and whipped it out of the loops. He laughed slowly, deep and calculating. He swung the belt over his head and aimed it at my naked body. The belt made a hissing sound as it sailed through the air before striking my bare skin. I screamed in pain and fell to my knees. He swung again, striking me across my back. Out of the corner of my eye, I saw Daniel lunge from the corner where he had been waiting. 'Don't even try it, Daniel,' Nick warned. His eye on Daniel, he hit me a third time. Turning to the others, he smiled and left the room.

I wept as I gingerly put on my clothes. I returned home, empty-handed once more, and refused to return to counseling. The counselor had told me to stand up for myself, be strong and I could accomplish anything. But when I had heeded her advice, I was beaten down. The bucket that held my hope was getting shallow and things were looking bleak. I could see no way out of this hell I was living in.

12

Kidnapped

I was dangerously weary. Tired of the nightly abuse, too sleep-deprived to keep up my grades in school, worried that the well-being of my brothers and my mum – even my dog – would be hurt or my dad's job ruined if I made a mistake. I was exhausted from hiding a hideous secret from my family, classmates, and boy-friend. I stopped writing letters to Jim. I stopped going to track practice. I sunk into a deep despair. My desire for life was vanishing.

One late night that early spring, around the time of my seventeenth birthday, I told Daniel that I had made a decision as we drove to a client's home. 'I can't do it. I can't take Jonathan's offer.'

Daniel stopped the car and stared at me dumb-founded. 'Are you crazy, Theresa? Do you know what he will do to you and your family if you refuse him?'

'It doesn't matter. I just can't. Please tell him for me.'

Daniel just shook his head and continued to drive.

I was starting to believe that Jonathan was the leader of something even more sinister than what I was experiencing. My one mysterious encounter with him led me to wonder what was really going on. I had seen and heard hints of confidential business dealings that seemed to involve high stakes. The expensive houses, clothes, jewelry and guns in addition to the amounts of money I'd seen lying around proved that the men weren't just working for their fathers' grocery stores. I suspected I was a pawn in a dangerous, mafia-type game. This was a life-or-death situation.

If I worked for Jonathan, I was certain that he would offer me to wealthier, more powerful men. They wouldn't be small-time guys like Nick; it would be a more dangerous game. Daniel didn't like the fact that I had told him no. He kept asking me if I was sure. Did I want to reconsider? My answer remained the same.

I was 'working' for Nick because I didn't have a choice. I was trying to keep my family safe until I had done enough to earn back the photos from Nick. The shame of being found out, the risk of my father losing his job if they leaked the pictures to his boss, the responsibility of keeping my brothers out of harm's way, all gave me no choice in the matter. I felt forced to see this through to the end, whenever that would be. But Jonathan wanted me to leave my family, to walk away from any chance of a normal life. It would mean no Sunday family dinners ever again. No college or career. No marriage or family with Jim. If I took Jonathan's offer, it would mean saying goodbye to all I had ever known or dreamed of. I would live in a nice apartment, service rich men while he grew rich, perhaps start doing drugs to cope, work in the strip club their family had ties with and eventually be sold off to an old foreign man and leave the country I had grown up in and loved. I couldn't voluntarily choose that path so I refused.

Soon, instead of me helping Daniel with his math homework, as I regularly did, he began asking me if I needed help with my homework. Even my Chaldean friends Bassim and Hassam sensed the change in me. They noticed the dark circles under my eyes and the speech papers that passed by their desks with my failing grades. They realized all they had taught me (a few Arabic words) would not be enough for my survival. There was a feeling of tension in the air, a brooding danger. The Michigan weather was cold one day and rainy the next. Spring tried to break through but to no avail. The dreary weather matched my spirit. Mechanically I went through the motions. By evening, I could no longer remember what I had done during the day. I wished, hoped, someone would care enough to intervene before I ended up dead.

Lying in bed one night, in total desperation, I got out and knelt down on the floor. I folded my hands and closed my eyes and sent out a prayer that the torture would soon be over.

'God, are you there? This is Theresa. Please, God, let me get the pictures back next time. Please keep my parents and brothers safe from harm. I love them. Send your angels to protect me. I need you, God. I can't hold on for much longer. In your name, I ask this. Father, Son, Holy Ghost. Amen.'

I was numb to all feelings and emotions except for when I prayed. Tears rolled down my cheeks when I drifted off to sleep. Hours later, I woke to the shrill sound of my phone. Sadly, I reached for the receiver. I didn't need to hear the message. I didn't need to guess what or who it was. I knew. 'Theresa, I need to meet you. We really have to talk,' Daniel said.

Groggily, I agreed. As if I had a choice.

'Things are about to change and you are in trouble. Can you meet me now?'

His words sent fresh fear coursing through my veins and I was instantly awake. I sensed that circumstances were about to get worse.

'What's wrong? What is happening? Daniel, I'm scared.'

'I know. I will explain in a little while,' he told me.

'You have to help me,' I pleaded.

'All I can tell you is that I talked to Jonathan.'

'I don't know how much longer I can do this,' I pleaded with him.

He sighed. 'Meet me in the usual place in ten minutes. This is the last time. I promise.'

Though it was growing cold outside, I didn't risk the noises of pulling open my dresser drawers and changing clothes. My dad was home and I had to be extra careful not to wake my parents. I quietly opened my bedroom door, as I had done so many times before, and crept past my parents' closed bedroom door. Sneaking down the stairs, I was careful not to make a single sound. After squeezing my pajama-clad body through the narrow space of the sliding glass door in the family room that seemed to have taken me forever to inch open, I turned around to look at the door as I slowly shut it, careful to leave a few inches open so I could get back in hours later. Barefoot, I tiptoed through my backyard. The cold dew soaked my feet as I snuck through the neighbor's yard, noticing the light on in their family room and the owner watching TV. I crouched behind the bushes so he wouldn't see me and quietly ran toward the street.

Under dim streetlights the neighborhood's houses were all quiet, the residents sound asleep. I never got used to waiting in this spot, waiting for the nightmare to begin all over again and never knowing if I would be returned to this very spot again later. Or not at all. Something felt odd tonight though. My stomach churned nervously; fear-induced adrenalin caused my heart to thunder in my ears.

I didn't have to wait long before the Trans Am approached. Maybe tonight I would be released from bondage. Maybe tonight they would give me the photos and leave me alone, I thought optimistically. As Daniel's car stopped in front of me, I felt the hairs on my arms stand straight up. I felt a tug on my shoulder, as if an angel was telling me not to go. It was dark and I leaned in to the passenger window to see who was in there. Arabic music played on the stereo but Daniel wasn't in the driver's seat.

'I thought Daniel was coming to talk to me,' I said nervously.

'Yeah, we know,' the unknown Chaldean man replied. 'We made him call you.'

'Where is he? This is his car.'

'He won't be able to help you tonight. Get in.'

Instinctively, I shrunk away from the car. Suddenly the car door opened and a strange Arabic man grabbed my waist and pulled me into the car. Fear surged through my veins as I struggled, trying to escape. I opened my mouth to scream, but a hand quickly shot out from somewhere, and struck me across the face. The blow made my head spin, and stars clouded my vision. The door slammed shut and tires screeched as the driver sped from the estate. The inside of the car was filled with the cruel laughter of the men. In shock it took me a while to focus on where we were going and the surroundings. After we had driven for a while, through the window I saw we were in an unfamiliar, dark, poverty-riddled area of Detroit. The landscape was dotted with abandoned buildings, boarded-up houses, and vacant lots. It smelled dirty.

Even if I escaped, where would I go? I had no idea where I was. I cried uncontrollably. Somehow, I knew my survival was threatened tonight. I could feel it in my body. I felt as if I was in another world, far from the comforts of my bedroom in my nice home. None of that mattered at this moment.

Above the loud music, the men spoke Arabic slang and laughed. I understood a few words here and there as the men talked a mixture of Arabic and English. The words 'fun', 'sex', 'money' and 'job' seemed to crop up often in the conversation. I heard Nick's name mentioned and I heard Jonathan's name too. Chills went down my spine. I was revolted by the combination of smells, their musky cologne mixed with sweat and the biting odor of alcohol on their breath. They passed around bottles filled with alcohol and someone pressed a bottle to my lips. I clenched my mouth tightly closed and was backhanded.

'Don't hurt her too much,' I heard one of them caution from the front seat. Gasping, I choked as burning liquid was dumped down my throat. 'We need her tonight. Besides, he'll be mad if you hurt her.'

The car slowed and pulled into the parking lot of a sleazy, dirty motel. There were broken-down cars in front of the doors to the rooms. I was half-carried, half-dragged into one of the rooms. It smelled of old cigarette smoke. I saw a large, king-sized bed and dresser. There was a mirror, several chairs and a table and about two-dozen Arabic men waiting for me. More nasty-tasting liquid was poured down my throat. It tasted different from the other liquid they had made me drink in the car. It was a familiar bitter flavor.

As I scanned the room, I saw the only two people I knew in the crowd – the evil Chaldean cousins – my traffickers. 'The present has arrived for some of you,' Nick announced to the men. 'The boss's way of saying thank you for a job well done. The rest of you, you can't have this prize possession tonight. You need to work harder for the family. But let this be an incentive of what you can have later!'

I was told to strip and stand on top of the flimsy motel-room table. When I tried to keep my underpants on, the room erupted with laughter and they were torn from me. I was examined by the men, all trying to get a good look as if I was a piece of meat at the butcher's. And then the bidding began. The price went higher and higher, though much of it I couldn't understand. Suddenly I was grabbed by unknown hands and shoved roughly to the bed. The first man paid Nick and was the first to get to use me. After that the bidding continued for the men who wanted the next turn. This went on and on, until I lost count of how many used my body while the others in the motel room watched, drank, talked and laughed. The fact that I was not there of my own free will excited them.

At some point during the night, I lost consciousness. I blacked out from the intense trauma overload and the liquor, which I believe was laced with some drug, being forced down my throat from time to time. Who knows what they did to me after that point or for how long. When I finally came round, my head was spinning and cloudy. I didn't want to open my eyes. I wanted to leave them closed for eternity. It was unusually quiet. Slowly opening my eyes, I struggled to focus. The room was empty except for empty beer cans and liquor bottles, and cigarette butts were strewn everywhere.

A wave of nausea caused me to bolt for the bathroom but as I got to my feet I doubled over as severe pain shot through my legs, my private area and my abdomen. I dropped to the floor, curled in the fetal position, gasping to breathe. Eventually I was able to get on my hands and knees and crawled to the toilet. There, I threw up violently. After rinsing my mouth, I washed my face with cold water at the sink. I left the bathroom and searched for my clothes, picking up the sheets and looking under the bed. Standing there, vulnerable and naked, I felt the rise of bile once again in my throat. I ran to the toilet. After I vomited the second time, I lay my head on the cold toilet lid in desperation. With my head facing the shower, I saw my clothes. They were in the bathtub, wet.

Part of me wanted to take a bath and soak my aching body. Had I been left in the rundown motel because they thought I was dead? Were they trying to keep me captive, knowing I had no way to return home? Were they forcing me to wait for them, for whatever future plans they had for me? I put on my cold, wet pajama pants and T-shirt. My underwear was long gone, most likely carried off as someone's souvenir from the night's activities. I needed to escape fast before someone returned. I opened the motel-room door and walked outside. The parking lot was dirty. Barefoot, wet and cold, my head was still cloudy and my stomach churned. I didn't know where to go. I had no money, no shoes, no identification, and no idea where I was. I didn't have anyone to call to come and get me. I had nothing.

I noticed a small diner was at the rear of the motel and I could see people were inside. Maybe someone would give me a ride home. Maybe there was a way out of this situation after all. Maybe Daniel would show up looking for me and take me back, I thought to myself at the sight of the place. Disjointed thoughts ran through my mind. *What a nasty place. Who would eat here? What if someone knows these guys and they come back for me? Should I hide?* Entering the lobby, I saw about six people sitting at booths, mostly old men, smoking, chatting and eating. A middle-aged waitress, who looked like she'd experienced many hardships too, walked between the tables, smiling at the customers and making small talk as she poured coffee. At that moment I would have traded my life for hers. No matter how big our house was or what a good family I had. Right now I would rather be in her shoes.

She caught my eye as I peered sheepishly through the lobby window. Dripping wet, without shoes and covered in bloodstains, I looked a mess. I had just turned seventeen, and was stuck somewhere within the depths of the slums of Detroit, somewhere between late night and early morning. Opening the door, she gave me a sympathetic look. 'Can I help you, sweetie?'

Wow. I was shocked. No one had ever asked me that before. It seemed I had waited for an eternity to hear those words. 'No, I don't have any money. I'm OK,' I stated proudly as I had been taught.

'Let me know if you change your mind,' she replied sweetly, not judging.

I sat on the cracked plastic cushioned bench in the tiny lobby of the diner and considered my options. I needed to get home. I could call my parents. Yet there was no way I could call home. Then my parents would finally know. My family's lives would be in jeopardy. A black car pulled up to the motel and I shrank down in the cushions. But it wasn't them. I resolved to call home – it felt like the only way to get back there. I motioned to the waitress and she came back out to the lobby. 'Could I borrow a dime? I need to make a phone call.' She nodded and pulled a coin from her apron pocket. She returned to her customers as I slid the dime into the lobby payphone.

My heart pounded in my chest as my shaking fingers pushed the numbers for my house. What time was it? As I heard the rings, I held my breath. A recorded message came on saying that I needed to first dial the area code. Where was I? My dime came back out. It must be long distance and I needed more money to make the call. I couldn't ask the waitress for more money so I knew I would have to make a collect call. I gave the operator my home number. It rang once, twice, three times. I became more frightened with each ring of the phone. My dad would be furious. 'Hello?' a man's voice answered groggily.

I slammed down the receiver before the operator could give him my name. I couldn't do this. Not after what I had just gone through. Not in the same night. To endure torture, and then disappoint the people who cared about me the most and put them in danger was more than I could bear. I rested my head on the side of the payphone and cried.

Glancing up, I noticed the waitress watching me and talking on the phone inside the restaurant. Now what? While I silently prayed, a police car pulled up outside the motel restaurant. The officer got out of the cruiser, walked up to the door and looked at me. I didn't know whether to be relieved or scared. I had never had dealings with police before. Perhaps he could drop me off at home. 'What seems to be the problem here, honey?' he asked nicely.

'I need to get home,' I answered. 'Can you give me a ride?'

'How old are you? Do your parents know you're out this late? Where do you live?'

I shrunk back from the pummeling questions. 'Um, I'm seventeen. I live in Birmingham. Could you just give me a ride?'

'Sure. Let's talk in the car on the way home.'

This might just work. He went inside and spoke with the waitress again and then talked on his walkie-talkie. The longer I waited, the more exhausted I became. It was a long time since I'd slept. 'Can you tell me what happened back there?' the officer asked when he got in the car and drove off. 'Why are you all the way out here?'

I had no idea where I was and had no intention of telling him how I got there so I pretended to sleep, occasionally mumbling an 'I don't know' to pacify him. I was in shock and could barely move the muscles of my mouth to respond. I was also worried about getting inside my house and into my own bed without any of my family discovering I had been out. All I wanted was to get in to a hot, soothing bath and soak away the aches, pains, blood and the awful odor of the cologne and body fluids of so many disgusting men.

'Who took you all the way here and left you? I really need you to tell me. Are you hurt? Do you want to go to the hospital?'

As I had learned to do at the counseling appointments, I remained silent. They can't do anything if I don't answer. All I wanted to do was get home. It was a long ride before the police cruiser pulled into my driveway. The big white pillars looked familiar yet ominous. It felt good to be home but I was terrified of my family finding out the truth. But then a desperate idea popped into my head.

As the policeman parked the car, I quickly got out. 'Thanks for the ride,' I said and hurried out.

I actually thought I could go around the back of the house, open the sliding glass door that was waiting for me, sneak back inside and go to bed. I thought I could get away without anyone knowing I had been out. Without anyone finding out about the multitude of rapes I had endured that night. And that I could still keep everyone safe.

But he turned off the car engine and followed me. The front porch lights turned on. Oh no. How was I going to get out of this one? The policeman was walking towards the front door and I knew it was over. By the time I reached the front porch, my parents opened the door and met me, clad in their pajamas, robes, and dark frowns.

Our dog ran into my arms. I gingerly bent to pick him up. 'Oh, Bowzer!' I held him tightly as he licked my swollen face. His unconditional love was a balm for my body and soul.

'Stay here while we talk to the officer,' my father said sternly.

They went into the living room as I waited for what seemed like eons. How could I continue to protect my family if the truth came out? Daniel said these guys meant business. Maybe I should have taken Jonathan's offer to keep my family safe. What would they do now that the police were involved? I was sure they were watching. How could I continue to do this without my family getting hurt?

As I sat waiting, images of all the times they had threatened me to remain quiet flooded my memory: *'If you tell anyone, we will kill your brothers. Your mum is home alone a lot too, isn't she?'*

I could see the cars following Pat and me as we walked home, the times I would go outside to get the newspaper and see a dark car with tinted windows parked down the street with the engine running. I recalled my trips to the mailbox to get the mail and the string of small dead animals that had shown up inside. I sat there and held our gorgeous puppy; I knew that the truth wasn't an option.

'Theresa Lynn.' My father summoned me to the living room.

My parents believed that I had been out all night partying and whoring around with boys. I didn't try to change their minds. I kept quiet and just agreed with whatever they said. Their minds were made up. Nothing I said could have changed the situation without putting us all in grave danger. And I wasn't about to try.

The officer studied me with knowing eyes. 'May I talk with Theresa, alone?' he asked.

My parents went to the kitchen to make coffee. Day was dawning. 'Theresa, I know what happened,' he said gently. 'I've seen this before. You're not the only one. I know you're not doing this voluntarily, like your parents think.' He leaned forward and looked at me seriously. 'Am I right?'

I kept my eyes to the floor as I was accustomed to doing but gave him the slightest indication of a nod. 'I can help,' he offered, 'but I need your help as well. We believe there is a large criminal ring involving a large group of Chaldeans. Does the last name Gerard sound familiar?'

My heart dropped into my stomach and I lifted my head to look at him. I stared into his eyes, not nodding or denying. It was the most I could offer as an affirmation without speaking.

'That's what I thought.' He pulled out a business card and handed it to me. 'Take my business card and call me when you're ready to talk. I need an insider in order to get to them. But you must realize that this is very dangerous.'

I found my voice at that moment and replied, 'No shit.'

He didn't act surprised by my sudden speech or vulgar words. 'We want to get the top guy,' he continued. 'Jonathan.' My eyes widened at his name and I swallowed. Noting my reaction, the officer nodded and left.

Zombie-like, I went upstairs, filled the tub with scalding hot water and stayed there for hours. My tears flowed like the water from the faucet as I attempted to wash away only God knew what from my body.

I missed school that day. Surprisingly, I was allowed to sleep right through to late afternoon. My mind, body, and soul screamed inside. Each time I woke, often from the pain, I closed my eyes again, preferring sleep to the harshness of reality. Late that afternoon, my brother's yelling woke me. My mum knocked on my bedroom door. 'Do you have Bowzer in there with you, Theresa?'

'No.'

'Get up and help us look for him. We can't find him.'

My three brothers and I combed the neighborhood, the estate, and the park. We made posters and hung them everywhere. The boys rode their bikes to the grocery store on the busy intersection. Patrick wanted to stop by the police headquarters to give them a poster. I stalled. I knew I was being watched. If I was seen going in to the police building, someone might think I was going to them for help for a different matter. I stood outside, waiting for my brothers to come back out.

Late that night, my private phone line rang. When I answered I heard a dog bark and a gunshot. I stifled a scream in my throat, not wanting my family to hear as tears streamed down my face. I hung up the phone and walked over to the desk in my room. I opened the drawer and took out the policeman's business card. I read the name on the card then tore it to shreds and threw it in the trashcan.

That night, I cried myself to sleep, knowing that even though I had kept my mouth shut, the danger wasn't over. I couldn't even protect my dog. The threat was obvious: if I spoke (the dog's bark), then someone would be dead (the gunshot). There appeared no way out.

After the police incident, I was grounded. It was ironic to be punished at home, but I didn't argue. I was relieved to hide in my room after school, trying to heal. I listened to my records over and over again: the Carpenters when I felt desperate, Air Supply when I missed Jim, REO when I dreamed of being normal, and ACDC when I allowed myself to be angry. I cried, wrote in my diary, and prayed. I prayed I wouldn't be called at night, now unable to get out of the house. I prayed this torture would end and I could be a normal teenage girl.

A few days later, as I was falling asleep, the phone rang. My heart stopped. 'Hello?' I said, tentatively.

'Theresa? This is Jonathan.'

I froze, unable to answer. In a panic, my eyes instantly went to the bin next to my desk to see if the policeman's business card was in there but it had already been emptied by one of my brothers.

'How are you feeling? I heard about what happened last week.'

What was I supposed to say?

'I could have protected you. You didn't have to go through all of that,' he said. 'If you agree to my conditions, I will guarantee things like that won't happen. You will be treated like a queen and I will personally select the people.' He paused. 'Theresa, those guys are dangerous. You might not live through this.'

I did not have the words to respond.

'I can make your life easier. You'll have your own nice little apartment, designer clothes, and all the money you could ask for.'

'I don't know,' I stammered.

'I'll get the pictures from Nick and make sure your family is protected. Think about it.'

The phone went dead. Stunned, I held the receiver in my hand for several minutes. Here was an exit, but it wasn't really a way out. It was getting in deeper. On the one hand, it seemed like I would be released from having to perform sex acts with Nick and his men. I would no longer be indebted and scared that my family would be harmed. But on the other hand I would be forced to leave my family, run away and be at someone's complete mercy, never knowing what was going to happen. My dreams of college and a normal life would never be realized. How would I escape this? Would Nick ever give up the photos? Ever give up his hold on me and the money he was making through me? My dad was up for another promotion, which meant a raise and relocation. Every two years it came like clockwork. But he also had co-workers who were told this was where they would stay. The company was trying to make cuts and not move their employees as frequently, as it was expensive for them. If he got that call, I would be stuck here and then what?

I couldn't last much longer. Emotionally and physically I was at the end of my ability to cope. I wouldn't live long if this continued. I had two options. Stay with the current arrangement and hope we relocated soon. Or accept Jonathan's proposition. Either way, I couldn't endanger my family.

Unable to concentrate in school the next day, I pondered the options. How would I stay alive? My parents were watching me as well as the Arabs. Should I submit to Jonathan? Hand over my life, what was left of it?

The phone rang during dinner the next night. My dad was supposed to be out of town but the trip had been cancelled. My parents didn't allow phone calls during dinner and my father was not happy about having to leave his meal and get up to answer the phone. 'Hello?' He frowned. 'Hello? Hello?' He hung up and returned to the table.

'Who was that?' my mother asked.

'I don't know. They hung up. But there was weird music in the background,' he said.

We resumed eating dinner. But I had lost my appetite. I couldn't help thinking that if they'd wanted to speak to me they would have called my private line. I knew it was another warning.

The threats continued more frequently from this time onwards. Each time I ignored the telephone or didn't pick it up when it rang in the night a dead bird, dead mouse or a black rose was left in our mailbox. A car sat outside my house for hours after following my brother and me as we walked home from school. The warning was clear and it was deadly.

People often say they wish to be rich and live in a large home but people living in those places can be miserable. My parents fought more than ever and I was afraid they were going to divorce. My dad stayed out late and my mum was unhappy.

One afternoon, my brother was not at our accustomed meeting spot to walk home with me. He was supposed to wait for me and I was angry that he hadn't. Maybe he went home sick from school, I reasoned. I liked his company; it made me feel safe even though I knew he couldn't do anything to help. Not really.

At home, I got a snack and sat down to watch television.

'Theresa,' my mum called later from the laundry room. 'Where's your brother?'

'I thought he was here already. He didn't walk home with me.'

'He didn't come home early. He left a note that he was staying late after school but he should be home by now. Check his room and see if he's there.'

Pat's bed was made and his room was neat as he always kept it, but he wasn't in his room. 'No, Mum,' I called down the stairs. 'He's not here.'

She drove to the school to see if she could find him while I waited for my other brothers to arrive home from school. The three of us rode our bikes around the neighborhood, searching for Patrick at the park down the street. My mum phoned my dad who was out of town on business. She called the police. After our dog disappeared, my parents were suspicious of the neighbors. I wondered if my brother going missing was another warning from the Chaldeans. I thought back over the week, had I answered the phone every time? Would they take my brother now, too?

I was growing more terrified by the moment but for different reasons than my mother. My brother was fragile and sensitive. He couldn't handle what I had experienced. I didn't doubt for a moment that these monsters would sexually abuse my brother just as they had done to me. I needed to protect him no matter what it cost me. I had to reach Daniel and keep this from my parents. But how? I had never called Daniel. He always called me. I didn't even have his phone number. The phone book was no help; there were two-dozen listings for his last name. I searched the listings until I found one that matched the name of his street. I'd once noted it in the early hours of the morning as he took me home.

I dialed the number. 'Hello? Hello?' I said when the line picked up.

'Ya? Ya?' The old woman had a thick accent.

'Can I speak to Daniel?'

The woman babbled in Arabic.

'Daniel, please!' I shouted into the phone. The line went dead. Then I heard shouting from Patrick's room.

'I found a letter,' my mum told us. 'In a notebook on his desk.'

'What does it say?' I asked.

She read the letter out loud. It said that he was unhappy about how people were treating him. He was running away to visit his godmother in California, a thousand miles away. My mum called my dad, one of her friends and our uncle who lived nearby. They talked to the police about where Pat was headed.

My mind raced. I was relieved my brother had not been kidnapped, but the situation confirmed that I still needed to protect my family. They couldn't handle my drama right now, too. I had to remain quiet and endure my nightmare until I figured some way out. Pat was gone several days before we found him and got to talk to him. My family was a mess. And I was determined not to add to their problems.

In the spring semester of my junior year, I took a typing class. It was my last class of the school day and I really enjoyed it. The class was off the same hallway as my locker. Randy, a cute Jewish boy whose locker was next to mine, was standing there. He was popular, smart, handsome, rich and we often joked around. With my back to the hall pulling out my notebook, getting ready for the typing class, I heard something change in Randy's voice as he spoke to me. I looked over at him. Randy stood frozen. Then I turned and saw Nick and his cousin.

'Get lost, kid.' Nick looked threateningly at Randy.

Randy looked at me apologetically, and then ran down the hall to class as the bell rang.

'I have to get to class,' I pleaded. 'I can't be late.'

'Do you really think we care, Theresa?' Nick

stepped closer. 'We need you after school for something very special.'

'I can't, Nick. My mum is expecting me home right after school.'

'It wasn't a request.' He backed me against my locker. 'Be there.'

As he reached for my throat, the typing classroom door opened and the teacher peeked out. 'Theresa, are you coming?'

'Yes,' I timidly responded while begging her with my eyes to help me and intervene. *Someone, please do something to stop this*, I silently wished.

'She'll be there when I'm finished with her.' Nick stepped toward her.

She stared at him, nodded her head, and with a terrified look turned and went back into the classroom, too afraid to confront them or demand that I return to class.

I was stunned as Nick and his cousin left, laughing down the hall. I opened the door to the classroom and slid inside to my seat. The teacher handed out a paper to copy on our individual typewriters. The room was silent except for the hypnotic sound of keys hitting paper. No conversations, just kids concentrating on placing their fingers in the correct positions and hitting the right keys. The teacher didn't look at me. Another person had let me down. I was happy that Nick and his sidekick hadn't hurt or embarrassed me but I was in shock to find yet another teacher who turned their back on the situation, timid and unwilling to step across the line. I realized she was also afraid of Nick. The teacher never spoke to me again for the rest of the school year.

After class that day, I wasn't surprised to see Daniel waiting by my locker. Randy was back at his locker but didn't look my way. Our joking around was over. I followed Daniel to the parking lot. As we neared his car, I saw my friend Janie near a fancy car with an older Chaldean guy. I recognized him – he was the man with the knife who'd raped me. He gave me an evil smile. Janie had been flirting with him, and speedily turned away when she saw me watching. No, no, I thought. Not her too.

Seated in Daniel's Trans Am I began, 'I can't do this anymore. This is the last time.'

'I know,' he said sadly. 'I don't know how you have survived this long.'

'They can give the pictures to my parents. I don't care.'

'OK. I will ask them again,' he said.

'Tell them. This is it. No more. I want the pictures. I've done more than enough to earn them, Daniel.'

'I might finally be able to convince them.'

We drove to a part of Detroit I had never been to

before. This was an upper-class neighborhood. Before the kidnapping, I would only be called into service in the middle of the night. I normally would be taken to Daniel's family home but I also went to homes in rich parts of town. But now that the police were watching and I was grounded and my parents were suspicious, they demanded I go with them after school or even during school. During daytime, I would be taken to unknown, unfamiliar places.

I was far from home, trapping me further and leaving me absolutely no options of escape until they were finished with me. Where I was or what I would be walking into was never known. The only thing I knew was that I would be manipulated and coerced into continuing to do this until my debt was paid and I could finally get the pictures back and ensure my family's safety. I would never get back Bowzer.

Daniel parked and he seemed more apprehensive than usual. The driveway was full of cars, never a good sign. I reached for the door handle, ready to get this over with and never do it again. Daniel laid his hand on my arm.

'Theresa,' he cautioned. 'Be careful. These aren't nice guys. They aren't like the others.'

If Daniel was apprehensive about this situation, then I knew this would be bad. I suddenly felt nauseous. But there was no turning back. There never was.

Daniel held my hand and led me through the garage and into the house. He held up a hand, indicating the need to be quiet as we entered the kitchen. He peeked around the corner and motioned me forward. We made our way down steep stairs to a finished basement, a den of desire. The main room was a bedroom, complete with a huge bed in the center and mirrors lining the walls and ceiling. In a separate section of the room there were low couches and a television. This 'lounging' room was filled with about seven or eight men waiting for Daniel and me.

Loud music played as the men watched Arabic television, smoked and drank. I had never seen these guys before and I sensed immediately that this was a scary situation. I was grateful that Daniel was with me, something they hadn't let him do lately. No one acknowledged my presence. I was nothing but an accessory or ornament. I meant nothing. I wasn't considered human. Nick appeared in front of me. 'Finally. We have been waiting for you. You're going to really like this.'

'Gentlemen,' he raised his voice to the room. 'This is a small token of our appreciation for all your hard work. Enjoy any way you wish.'

I nudged Daniel.

'Nick, she wants the pictures,' Daniel said. 'She feels she has done enough.' Neither firm nor convincing, Daniel eyed his cousin.

'Let's see how she does today,' Nick told him, not looking at me.

There was a glimmer of hope I'd not seen before. Did Janie have anything to do with this? Perhaps she was being prepped to take my place, I thought.

I was surprised that Daniel's quiet cousin started off first. He had only taken me twice in the past two years. He usually sat in the corner and enjoyed watching. He stood first and pointed to the bed. I walked over and he took me while some men watched television in the adjoining room and others drank and smoked leaning next to the bed watching. In the beginning, he was gentle. He spoke to me in Arabic and told me to put my hand on his genitals and then told me to rub him. I understood a few words and obeyed the first command. But I didn't understand the last word of the second foreign request. He knew I could understand some words but was testing me to see how fluent I was becoming. He had tricked me. Either irritated with my lack of comprehension or wanting to look good in front of the others he slapped my face and the men in the room erupted in laughter.

'I told you what to do,' he demanded. 'Now listen or there will be more.'

I was shocked and looked over at Daniel in the corner watching intently. I knew he couldn't do anything to help me. When the cousin saw me look to Daniel he grabbed my legs and brutally pulled them open, now angry at me for turning towards Daniel. After he finished, I wanted to curl into a ball and recover. Immediately the next man left the television, took off his clothes and ordered me to get on my knees. This went on for hours.

I knew enough Arabic to know the men were teasing Daniel, trying to make him take a turn as well. He ignored them but they were relentless. He didn't have much control over what happened to me but he was Jonathan's little brother so he was safe. No one could touch him, not even Nick. The look on his face suggested his own torture was that he continually witnessed me getting tied up and being hit, and that he repeatedly watched my limbs being yanked apart. But I did wonder if he did care about me or if this was just an act.

When I thought they were finally finished, when I could barely focus, barely remember what I had come for, an extremely large Chaldean man stepped forward. He was not like the cultured, expensively dressed Arabs who reeked of money and power. He was huge and sloppy and didn't seem dangerous at all. He seemed perfectly harmless, I thought. By now, though, all the men had been drinking for the past few hours and wanted to watch this big guy take me. 'Kneel down!' he demanded.

He unbuckled his pants and let them drop to the floor. He grabbed my head and shoved it roughly to him and ordered me to commit an oral sexual act on him. I obeyed as other Arabs wandered into the room to laugh mockingly at this spectacle. He must have been over 300 pounds and he liked the attention he was getting. He kept his hand on top of my head and would not remove it, even as I started to choke.

Disgusted at what I was being forced to do and tired from brutal physical and sexual abuse, I reached my breaking point. My head was reeling and I could feel the bile rise in my throat. I reached up and tried to remove his hand from my head. I needed air. I was suffocating and about to be sick. He grabbed my hand and cruelly twisted it behind my back while pulling my hair as another man came up from behind and assisted him to keep me from moving. I was immobilized and my eyes searched the room for Daniel. I found him and with my eyes begged him to help me. But he sat in the corner of the room motionless with a look of terror on his face.

At the point of tears and struggling to breathe, I started to gag just as the large man was finished with me and I instantaneously vomited all over this grotesque man. Angry at what I had done he kicked me in the stomach and threw me to the side of the room. I landed hard on the floor, my head hitting the wooden dresser. The men's laughter filled the room mocking the large man, which angered him even more. Then he kicked me again in the stomach, his 300 pounds fully impacting into my slender body. Over and over he kicked me, until, huddled in a fetal position, I no longer moved. Bored, the men returned to their drinks and the television. Finally, the ordeal was over.

Daniel cleaned me up and helped me dress. My abdomen ached and I could barely stand.

Nick approached us. 'You earned this today.' Laughing, he threw a photo at my feet.

I don't remember the ride home. But I do remember clutching the picture in my hand, holding it close to my chest, cherishing the prize possession so dearly that I had bought with my body and soul. Back home I ran a hot bath and washed the fluids of other people from my body. I felt thankful to be home, thankful to be alive and thankful to have a photo.

As I sat in the bath I thought to myself, I have to get out of town without them suspecting before they carry out Jonathan's plans to keep me as his personal concubine. This is a battle for my life.

As time had gone by, I'd learned more Arabic and started to understand more about the plans being made by Jonathan. I knew he was arranging an apartment for me, planning to cut me away from Nick's business to create his own enterprise with me – more elite, more exclusive and more money. Now that I had been primed and prepared, they thought I was ready. All of this was being arranged despite the fact that I had said no.

There was an air around Jonathan. I felt the terror and intimidation he held over people. He embodied power and control and money. He was the head of a Chaldean mafia. I had no idea what to expect from him but I sensed something monumental was about to happen. I just didn't know what or how to stop it.

13

Hope at last

Late one Friday evening in the spring of 1982, my dad returned happy after a long business trip. He seemed joyous. It had been a long time since anyone in our home had been in high spirits.

My brothers were gathered in my room where we were playing the record player loudly. The Carpenters were followed by *Grease* and we sang along. We were all having a fun time. 'What do you think is up?' I asked my brothers.

'Maybe we're moving again,' one suggested.

'We couldn't be that lucky,' I retorted.

At dinner, Dad announced that the next day, Saturday, we would go out for dinner to a fancy restaurant. 'Cancel any plans you have for tomorrow and wear something nice,' he said.

The next day, we piled into the van and headed off for a long drive. All the way there, my brothers and I tried to guess where we were going. 'Have we been there before?' I asked.

'Will you give us a clue?' Michael asked.

'Tell us where we're going!' said Pat.

'No. No. No,' our parents answered each time.

Finally, we arrived at a beautiful mansion that also served as a restaurant. Our old van looked out of place among the Lamborghinis and Mercedes. Shyly my brothers and I followed my parents inside, feeling uncomfortable as we rarely went out to dinner, yet excited to see the exclusive, upscale restaurant. Taking a family of six out to eat wasn't cheap and we had never been to such an expensive place before.

We were seated and to our delight had our own personal butler. My younger brothers enjoyed sipping their drinks and then watching as the butler refilled their glasses after each sip. Servers brushed breadcrumbs off the table with a knife onto a small china plate.

'Order whatever you want,' Dad told us.

'I want a cheeseburger,' my youngest brother declared.

'When we go to fast food places you ask for shrimp,' Patrick observed. 'Now we're at a nice restaurant and you want a cheeseburger?'

Everyone laughed. It felt good to laugh.

When our meal was nearly finished and we had sufficiently irritated the waiter my dad cleared his throat. 'I have some very important news.'

'We know, Dad, what is it?' I asked impatiently.

'Yeah, Dad,' Patrick piped up. 'Tell us.'

'Who knows how to spell Connecticut?' he asked. Each of us took a turn but didn't get it correct.

'You're going to have to do better than that! We can't live in a place you can't spell, can we?' Dad said. We stared at one another, dumbfounded.

This would be my ninth move by the age of seventeen. As the news sunk in, all eyes were on me. Everyone assumed that I wouldn't want to move in my last year of high school to start all over again and make new friends. They thought I would be really upset, like I had been at the last move, and they nervously wondered what my reaction would be.

'Great!' I grinned. 'How soon can we go?'

My family stared at me, incredulous.

'Are you sure, Theresa?' Mum leaned forward. 'This means you will have to leave in your senior year.'

'It's a really good move for me,' Dad hastened to add. 'It means moving to the company's headquarters. We'll be near New York City and the beach.'

'Dad, really, I can't wait to go.' I glanced around the table at each of the family members. 'I've moved before, we are experts at it, right? This will be great!'

Surprised, everyone was silent for a moment. Then they all began talking at once. As my dad went on and on about the opportunities on the East Coast, the many things we could do and see, my thoughts drifted off.

I'll finally get out of this. It was my chance to get away. I could finally be free from the years of torture. Maybe I had a chance at life after all. And my family would never need to know what I went through for them. I just wish we still had Bowzer. That night when the phone rang after dark, I didn't answer it. Knowing my days of torture were numbered and freedom was near, I stood up for myself and went back to sleep.

I woke up feeling whole the next morning, instead of the usual empty feeling I had lived with for such a long time. I was energized with the knowledge that we were moving far away from here. I was finally going to be free. Over the last few weeks I had started to no longer care if my parents found out. I had started not to care if my captors carried out the numerous threats they kept making. I started to think that maybe I really could go to the police but with this latest news I would try escaping first.

To cope, to survive the unending horrific demands, I had closed down my emotions. That morning, as I studied my reflection in the mirror, I realized I had been living in a zombie-like numbness. I had been going to school, walking through the motions of my daily life, maintaining friendships and a long-distance boyfriend and wondering every day if I would be summoned to perform and where I would be taken. As I brushed my teeth each morning, dreading going to school I dreaded, I searched for an excuse to get out of what may come each day.

But today was different. I would stop it today. Whatever the cost, it would be the last day. But first I had to take care of some business. I needed to make sure someone else was protected and wouldn't be hurt when I left this place. With my shoulders straight for a change I walked to school with my brother, feeling closer to him than ever. As I walked I swallowed against a lump in my throat.

I had sociology class with my friend Janie that afternoon. I waited anxiously all day to talk to her alone. I'd noticed even more Chaldeans around her lately. I suspected that she was the reason why things were quieter for me. I hadn't been called as much since the vomiting incident a few weeks ago. Perhaps they were priming her to take my place. The thought disgusted me. I had to protect her. I couldn't let this happen to someone else.

'Janie, what are you doing after school?' I asked.

'I have plans,' she hedged. 'Why?'

'Wanna come to my house and hang out?' I replied.

'I can't. My mum is at work and I have to watch my little brother when he gets home from school,' she said. 'But you can come to my house.'

'Great. I'll walk with you.'

Shy and quiet, Janie was a sweet kid. I liked to do things with her. Because her parents were divorcing, her mum had to work full-time and therefore Janie watched her brother after school. Though she was plain she had a nice body. Unaccustomed to male attention, she hadn't ever had a boyfriend. With her father gone and her mum working full-time, she had little supervision. Janie was vulnerable – perfect prey for the Chaldeans.

As we walked to her house after school, making small talk, I noticed that she kept looking over her shoulder. When we got to her house we ate snacks and listened to records. It was nice to laugh again like a normal teenager. The pressure was easing off me, I was leaving this place soon.

'Are you dating anyone?' I asked. 'The Chaldean I saw you with a while ago?'

'So what if I am?'

'Janie! I can't believe it. Not you! Please be careful!' I pleaded. 'You don't know what you're getting your-self into. They are very dangerous!'

'You're wrong, Theresa,' she argued. 'He loves me. He wouldn't hurt me. He will protect me from the others. He told me.'

'Janie, these guys make you do things you don't want to. They will hurt you—'

'You should go, Theresa. They warned me that you might try to convince me not to go out with him, that you would say things to me. I'm not even supposed to talk to you.'

'Oh, Janie,' I groaned. 'They will suck you in. They will hold something over your head so you—'

She marched over to the hall and opened the door. 'Goodbye, Theresa.'

I walked home in despair. Janie was already involved with the Chaldeans and had no idea what her future held. I longed to keep her from the same fate as me. I phoned her many times after that before I left. I tried to talk to her in class. I wrote her notes during school but she wouldn't read them. It crushed me to watch Janie get into their cars after school, knowing what was happening to her. As the weeks progressed, I watched her spirit shrivel and die. I tried to save her, the way I wished someone had tried to save me. I was leaving soon, but she would be stuck here. My nightmare had become hers.

Even now I have attempted to locate Janie on a class-mate location website and through social-media sites but to no avail. Perhaps she got married and changed her name or moved far away like I did. Perhaps she didn't survive the ordeal she most surely faced after I escaped. About fourteen years ago I passed through Detroit and picked up a daily newspaper. There was an article about an upper-class white girl in her early twenties who had disappeared and was later found murdered. There were rumors that she had been secretly dating an Arab or Chaldean man and I knew her fate could have been mine. It made me think again of Janie and wonder just how many girls were victimized in this way. The appetites of these evil men were unquenchable. I had been one of the lucky ones, I escaped, but so many others don't.

I left with only two pictures in return for the two years of abuse and have no idea how many were taken the afternoon of the first rape. There is a high probability that other photos were taken during the horrific nights and afternoons of hundreds of men taking turns. I think they let me go because the police were involved. They were aware that the police were suspicious. They had no idea if I had been in touch with the police or what I had told them, and they weren't willing to sacrifice their entire operation and financial situation for one girl. No matter how much time they had taken to groom me it was easier for them to get another girl and start all over.

My escape was different from most girls' but my story is different from most too. Each of us has similarities in our stories and each of us is unique. Some of us were rich, some poor; some black, some white; some had two-parent families, others are from families that were broken and dysfunctional; some had abusive parents or parents that abused alcohol or drugs. I was lucky and escaped by moving. Many aren't as lucky. Still, I kept the details vague and was careful not to let many people know I was leaving. Most of all I didn't want the news getting back to Nick or Daniel. I knew the importance of keeping us safe, even hundreds of miles away.

My dad said that the house he had put an offer on was in negotiation because the couple was divorcing. It had to go to court first, and then it would be ours. It had a built-in pool and large yard. An hour from New York City, we'd be close to the beach. My family was excited. I was excited for a completely different reason. I knew that at last my personal hell was almost over. This move was my ticket out; my ticket to freedom.

There has been much discussion as to whether or not my story is one of human trafficking. Experts agree that, had this been caught today, it would qualify as a human-trafficking case. While it could also be considered child sexual exploitation, it does meet the definition of trafficking or domestic sex trafficking of a minor. It just isn't the typical depiction of a trafficking scenario.

As difficult as it was to escape, healing proved more difficult. The scars will last a lifetime as I learn to live with these gaping wounds in my heart.

Once we were safely in Connecticut I woke up early every morning in our summer beach house and walked down the quiet side street. I would walk past four houses, including the summer home of a famous author, and through the gate. Leaving the pavement behind, I'd step onto the sandy beach and face the Long Island Sound waters. The waves would roll towards me, welcoming me with their song as they climbed the sand to my feet.

A giant rock occupied a place on the community beach. Standing there like a sentry, and smooth from years of saltwater tides, the rock seemed to invite me onto its high recesses. Sitting with my legs crossed and my eyes closed, I listened. I felt the sun warm and purify my skin and I prayed. Mostly I thanked God for allowing me to be there. The tears that rolled down my cheeks were tears of relief. I was thankful for this second chance at life but sad for the young girl who was most likely taking my place back in Detroit.

Devastated by what I had endured, I hoped I could

reassemble my shattered soul and be a normal teen-ager once more. Could I possibly enjoy my senior year of high school harboring this secret? Could I truly put it all behind me? I spent three months on the beach, walking, healing and praying. I swam with my brothers during the day, went crabbing with my family, enjoyed crab bakes back at the beach house and read novels on the screened porch at night, the cool air brushing my neck. And I lied to myself that now it was over, I could forget and move on with the rest of my life.

By the time we left the beach community and moved into our stunning new home, I felt as if I could do it. I started my senior year of high school telling myself I was a good girl, pretending it had all never happened and that I was still a virgin. No one ever had to know. When I met a boy in school who was sweet and had no expectations, I told him I was a virgin. Mark never knew any different because he never tried anything physical. It was perfect. By dating Mark, I got into the popular group. He was in a band and even though he was very shy, he was very talented. I also joined the band, was accepted into color guard and learned routines throwing and swinging the large, colorful flags to the music. We traveled around and performed and for the first time in my life, I started to feel normal.

I tried out for a theatrical performance put on by the high school and made it through the auditions. I got a part-time job a mile away from my house at a little Italian restaurant and loved talking to people who worked at the factory across the street. Life was good. I tried to forget the past and put it behind me.

Whenever I remember what I tried to hide I felt better when I thought about water. We had a swimming pool in our backyard and I would get up when I couldn't sleep and do laps. I swam in the morning to start my day and after my shifts at work.

I rejoiced that I had escaped. I had survived the depths of hell. The healing process was underway. I was safe. My family was safe.

No one knew a thing until college, when it all came crashing down on me.

14

You can run but you can't hide

After I escaped the heinous abuse I miraculously resumed a normal teenage life. On the outside anyway. Hidden hundreds of miles from my abusers, I graduated high school, and then went away to college.

I was accepted 'on probation' to one college out of the three that I had applied to. Though I had excelled in my senior year of high school, and was even in 'honors' classes, my grade point average from the previous two years was so low that it was impossible to bring it up to an average college acceptance level. I had also failed horribly my college entrance exams. I had taken the entrance exams in the middle of my living hell in Detroit. I was told that these tests and your GPA were supposed to be indicators, a 'picture of your college success'. I had to beg for a chance to show them I had what it took to be a successful college student. Several years later I would graduate with a 3.35 GPA (out of 4) and later go onto obtaining a Masters degree. So much for that 'picture'.

My parents demanded that I attend a college two hours away from home. They said this way I would get the 'full college experience'. My boyfriend at the time, Mark, was staying at home and attending a Catholic college. I think they just wanted one less kid at home and if I was far enough away, it would make it difficult to come home every weekend. So in August of 1983 when I was eighteen years old, I left home and started college at Eastern Connecticut State University located in the little New England town of Willimantic. I shared the main floor of an old, blue, four-story Victorian house with three other girls. Upstairs were four college guys whom we bonded with, partied with and hung out with. We helped them pick out clothes for dates, taught them to cook food and signed for the numerous, mysterious packages that came in the mail for them regularly.

On the evenings that the packages would arrive, we all gathered in a large circle on the dusty, mangy couches and recliners and ate pizza. The oldest guy in the group, who had been a senior for several years, had a large balance scale on the ugly wooden coffee table in the middle of the room and weighed out various amounts of marijuana while the other guys bagged them up. Bruce Springsteen and the Grateful Dead played on the stereo while they took turns sampling the newest shipment and passed the joints around the circle. I always passed them on to the next person, never giving into the peer pressure to partake. 'Come on T, take a hit!' they would cheer.

'No, I'm fine really. I'll just grab another beer,' I replied each time.

I have never had the desire to do drugs of any kind but, like my parents, I found my refuge in alcohol instead. I drowned my sorrows, loneliness and fears until I would pass out unconscious, only to be awoken by hideous, vile nightmares. Screaming, night sweats and migraines followed these nightly episodes. I had physically escaped the men but they haunted me at nighttime when I was unable to escape.

My first two years of college seemed like a series of falling in and out of consciousness. I was somehow able to shine academically, making it to class most days. I loved my Spanish class and was a leader in the sociology course I took. But several nights a week, I was going to the only bar in town with friends, drinking pitchers of beer and whiskey sours. I would go home with men I didn't know, wake up around 3 or 4 a.m., terrified and naked, and find my clothes scattered around a stranger's dark room. I would run home to my rented apartment and fall fast asleep, exhausted. These incidents were flashbacks to my earlier years, repeating themselves over and over again, and I had no idea how to break the cycle.

During those two years at college, I ended up in the emergency room many times. I would drink so much that I would have panic attacks. My heart would race, my blood pressure would spike and I felt as if I was having a heart attack. Numerous times, I would be transported in an ambulance and taken to the small town hospital. The nurses would do an EKG, give me an IV with saline for dehydration and release me several hours later. No one ever asked about my mental state or emotional well-being or suggested counseling or alcohol rehab. I was seen as just another privileged college student who had simply drunk too much and couldn't handle their alcohol. Not someone who had PTSD – post-traumatic stress disorder – and was calling out for help.

The only way I knew how to relate to men was through sex. It gave me a temporary, and false, sense of power over them. I never felt worthy of a loving, long-term relationship. I felt too broken inside for anyone to possibly want me. Yet I still deeply yearned for that connection, for unconditional love that I had never known. For a protector, a human savior, in case those men returned for me some day.

In college, I never slept with guys then spent the whole night with them. I made up excuses to leave early because I felt I couldn't trust them and feared they might do something to me in the middle of the night when I slept. They might kidnap me or force me into a prostitution ring. I also didn't want them to hear my screams from my nightmares. I would jerk so hard in my sleep that I would smash my hand on the wall or the bedpost and wake up in pain. Sometimes I even woke up on top of my mattress on the floor, separate from the bed and box springs. I must have thrashed around so hard that it came right off the bed.

As I got older, I realized that this wasn't a healthy view on sex. I desperately wanted to get back my morals. I would meet a guy and be determined not to have sex with him. It felt good. I could concentrate on just him and me. But as our feelings grew stronger for each other, I got scared and would jump into bed with him to drive him away from a real relationship with me and turn it into a sexual arrangement. It was safer that way. I knew what to expect. People got hurt when they trusted and loved. Bad things happened.

Though my time on the beach and my calm senior year of high school had allowed me time to heal my body and my soul, I hadn't come to terms with my sexual foundation. I was a virgin when I was raped. I lived two long years without the ability to say no to sex.

I had no control over when a man wanted to have me. Sexuality and promiscuity surrounded college life, and for many it was their expression of freedom and experimentation. My world spun out of control. I lacked the emotional strength and relationship experience to say no. Without this power, many victims of sexual abuse deal with their past by either turning completely away from any sexual activity or becoming overtly sexual. I'd done the latter and I needed help.

At Christmas time, in the middle of my sophomore year of college, my parents told us that we were moving again. 'Your dad got transferred to Indianapolis. His job at headquarters is finished and they need him in the Midwest.'

'But I'm still in college. I can't just leave in the middle of the year!' I exclaimed. 'And Patrick is in his senior year of high school! This is just crazy!' I said in despair. A sense of sadness, shock and abandonment washed over me. My family would be a thousand miles away from me, but I couldn't move again. This was about my future. I was almost twenty years old. 'I am not going!' I said. 'Not this time. I need to stay somewhere more than two years and want to finish college at one school. I am old enough now. Is that too much to ask for?' I fought back.

So they moved six states away and I was left with

no car, no doctor's office, nowhere to have my birthday dinner, nowhere to spend Easter, and all my family were a thousand miles away. Mark helped me out occasionally but he lived two hours away, worked full-time and was in college too. We talked on the phone several times a week; he was the only person I talked to who had known me for even a few years. Yet he had no idea of what I was going through, physically or mentally. He had no idea of the demons I slayed each night I slept, the ways I was trying to cope and the struggles I was enduring. His family let me spend Easter at his house but it felt strained. It was unsaid but I am sure they thought, 'What kind of parents would leave their only daughter alone for the holidays?'

All the years that I was enslaved I hadn't had regular periods and I never used birth control. I didn't have sex after I moved away from Michigan until I got to college. Even in college, I rarely used protection because it was difficult to obtain (other than condoms) and I tried the Pill but it gave me horrible headaches. Sometimes, if I had extra money or if I remembered, I would use a barrier contraceptive with spermicide called the sponge, which was later taken off the market. I didn't use protection because I wanted to get pregnant, far from it. I believed I *couldn't* get pregnant. After having been raped thousands of times as a teen and never once having conceived, I felt that I would never be able to have children.

My wake-up call came as a surprise. As most do, I suppose. When I was nineteen years old, having started college the year before, I lived in a co-ed house and a few guys upstairs had formed a college bowling team with me and some of my roommates. I quickly developed a close friendship with one of the guys, Bobby. He was nice-looking and quiet and I regularly gave him advice on his girl problems. We had lots of long talks and on several occasions we ended up spending the night together, staying up late playing cards and drinking excessively. For some reason I felt safe with him and he was the first person I had ever slept with all night long. But when I woke up the morning after, I always slipped away before anyone was up and tiptoed quietly downstairs to my room. We vowed each time it happened that this would be the last time and for some reason we both felt as if it could never be permanent. I didn't feel worthy of being loved like that and felt he wasn't a strong enough man to protect me in the waking hours.

The following year I was a sophomore in college and we both lived in separate places but would occasionally run into each other. As time had gone on things had changed and I missed the days when we'd been together. In February, a month or so before spring break, all the students were joyfully anticipating warm weather, relief from studies, trips to exotic lands or home-cooked meals with family. I ran into Bobby in a bar one night and we spent hours reminiscing about the previous year over too many drinks and ended up going to his new apartment on campus where we had sex and spent the night together.

A month later I started getting dizzy and really nauseous. I couldn't eat or drink anything without being sick. I couldn't get out of bed because my whole body was exhausted. I hoped I had the flu but knew deep down it wasn't the flu because I didn't have a fever, a stuffy nose, not even a cough. I dragged myself out of bed, walked to the drug store and purchased a pregnancy test. It confirmed my worst nightmare: I was pregnant. I was stunned. This was impossible. Why now, after all these years? I panicked and thought of my parents' reaction. An all-too-familiar feeling from so many years earlier rushed back to me – when I was fifteen, being ashamed and not wanting to disappoint them. I immediately walked to Bobby's apartment and knocked on the door.

'Hey there, do you have a couple minutes? I need to talk to you,' I said as he opened the door.

I had never visited his place during the day. He was busy studying for mid-terms, packing to go home for spring break and seemed preoccupied. 'Sure, I have a few minutes. What's up, T? You OK?' he replied, surprised at my sudden visit. He knew me well and sensed my apprehension.

'No. I am not OK. I'm pregnant!' I blurted out as we walked into the apartment.

He stopped walking, dead in his tracks and turned around to face me. 'Holy shit!'

Bobby was a real gentleman. I told him honestly that I had only been with him that month. He accepted that it was his child and never questioned if it was true or not. I had come to him for help and that was enough for him. We discussed the options. We were both determined to graduate college and we were not in love. We mutually agreed to terminate the pregnancy, which he paid for and he took me to the appointment. He held my hand as we waited for our turn in the waiting room and people thought he was my boyfriend. He showed me kindness and tenderness in my moment of desperation. I was in shock. How could God let this happen to me? I was convinced I was sterile after the years of unwanted men entering me and never getting pregnant. I felt so confused.

I stopped drinking and became determined that I needed to change my life. Even though I knew I wasn't ready to be a mother at twenty years old, I was still devastated at the loss of the child growing inside me. It felt that this was God's way of waking me up. I had been given another chance at life. I told myself that those men had controlled me from the time I was fifteen until that moment, but not for a moment longer. I wouldn't and couldn't let them control me for the rest of my life.

My thoughts of change were confirmed several days after the abortion when I had a massive hemorrhage and could have died. Infection took over my body that was trying to heal from the invasive procedure and I spiraled into a state of haziness while I was drugged and slept. I dreamed of a new life where I had a career helping others and having a family someday. I woke from the fog and started to actually believe that I deserved to have a life like that. Now all I needed to do was try to figure out how to manifest those dreams and make them a reality.

After the end of the spring semester my parents flew me to their new home. I purposely left all my belongings in my apartment with every intention to return after summer and start my junior year of college. They had moved to a small country town outside of Indianapolis and the massive house had a game room with a bar, card table, pool table and ping-pong table. My mum showed me to my new room but something didn't feel right. I thought that perhaps the odd feeling was due to the fact that although all my familiar furniture from childhood was there, I hadn't packed it, nor had I been there to move it. But as I looked in the corner of the bedroom, I noticed a large, wooden, cedar chest with a beautiful upholstered top. It was stunning. I had always dreamed of having a Hope Chest, a place to hold a young girl's dreams, dishes, mementos and things to take with her into her marriage.

'If you stay here in Indiana you can have it,' my mum said, looking pleased with herself. She walked out of the room and said over her shoulder, 'But if you go back and live in Connecticut, you can't take it with you.' I was shocked. Was she really blackmailing me?

They knew I was only home for the summer and had plans to return to college in the fall. I strongly felt that I needed to break the cycle of moving every two years. I didn't really want to return to Connecticut with the bad memories, mistakes of my actions, the poor choices I had made and the loss of a baby. But while I needed the support of my family I also wanted to stand on my own two feet, start over and get strong.

I looked around the room again in disbelief and still felt uneasy. Something was missing. My coveted perfume bottle collection that I had had for over ten years wasn't there. All the beautiful, uniquely shaped bottles that my grandmothers had given me while growing up, all the bottles I had found hidden and forgotten at garage sales, auctions and flea markets, were missing. 'Mum!' I screamed in panic. 'Where is all my stuff?'

'Oh Theresa, we had to consolidate and I didn't think you wanted all of those old things anymore. I donated them to the Salvation Army.'

I began frantically searching for the rest of my belongings. My journals, fuzzy tie-dyed slippers, stuffed animals that my brothers had given me and Jimmy had won for me at carnival. Everything that held sentimental value, all was gone.

'How could you? Those things meant a lot to me. They all had a special meaning too. Why didn't you ask me?' I cried.

A new realization hit me full force. I had left all my belongings back at my college apartment and had come to what was supposed to be *home* and had ended up with nothing.

'Oh Theresa. They are just material objects. They aren't important. Family is what matters the most,' Mum replied like it was no big deal, subtly emphasizing again that I needed to move home.

I collapsed across the canopied bed in my bare, stark bedroom and cried uncontrollably until it was time to go downstairs for the family dinner. Once again I felt all alone in the world.

As the summer wore on my parents told me a thousand times that they didn't want to pay for out-of-state tuition for me for two more years of college and also had to pay for another kid in college now. They pressured me to go along on the college visits with my brother Patrick to 'help him know what to look for'. On each tour, I was persuaded by my dad to fill out an application to the college 'to just see what happens'. Once again I was trying to please everyone but I also yearned to have a say on this new chapter of my life. I tried to fight against what seemed like a predestined life of moving every couple of years and starting all over each time.

I ended up being accepted into Purdue University, Ball State University and Indiana University and ultimately succumbed to the pressure and chose to move back and stay in Indiana. At the beginning of the junior year in college I moved back to the Midwest. I began to see this as an opportunity to start afresh and finally get my head on straight. My parents paid a huge sum to a removals company that went to my apartment and loaded up all my belongings and transported them to our house in Indiana. Surprisingly, Mum and Dad never once complained about the cost. But once again I felt assaulted as unknown men went into my room touching my things without me being there and having to trust that all my things would end up at my new home.

In the fall when I was twenty my brother and I went off to college, moving into the dorms. I was accepted as a candidate for the social work department and was at the top of my class. I took this time to dry out from alcohol on my own and worked on healing my body, but the nightmares still haunted me. Learning how to heal my emotional body would take years, but while at college I learned another coping mechanism besides alcohol. Running.

Instead of drinking and going to parties, I began running again. I could control my life and memories during the day. But at night, when the nightmares woke me, I ran. I knew I was tempting fate by running late at night on a college campus but I was willing to take this risk. At the same time I was scared to death, yet felt as if nothing worse could ever happen to me during my lifetime. I always ran to the same place, a little church a few miles from my dorm. Even after midnight, in the pitch dark, the door was always open. Quietly, I slipped inside, basking in the peace and security that always welcomed me. This was the one place where I felt loved and accepted. I prayed; I cried. Then, exhausted physically and emotionally, yet happy, satisfied and content, I returned to the dorm and slept like a baby.

During this time, I noticed a boy called Mike who

lived in my dorm. I was drawn to his self-confidence. Mike walked down the dorm hall with his head held high, easily making eye contact with everyone, knowing what he wanted and what was right. He would wear sneakers with a suit and not care what anyone thought of it. He wasn't influenced by what other people said or by the dictates of society. Serious, driven and level-headed, he reminded me of his idol David Letterman.

Bubbly and outgoing on the outside, I shook with fear on the inside. I forced myself to hold up my head in order to be aware of my surroundings, to make sure I was safe and see who approached me. I conformed to the rules, a product of my upbringing, well aware of the consequences if I did not please others. Unlike Mike, I cared too much about what others thought of me. For this reason I was drawn to his energy. At last here was someone I felt safe with, someone strong enough to protect me. We got close and started a relationship that was both comforting and exciting. We were best friends and lovers. He taught me to trust and to allow myself to be loved. The relationship allowed me to begin to survive in a healthy way.

As Mike and I got closer and closer I realized I could no longer hide my past from him. I had explained away my skittishness when men walked by in the dark or in intimate situations. But I was finding it a difficult internal balance between allowing him to love me, lowering my emotional walls and always remembering, always feeling afraid and never fully trusting anyone. It tore me up inside. It got to a point where I could no longer cover it up. It was a double-edged sword. I wanted to tell him but was he strong enough to endure my secret? Was his love for me secure? Or would he turn and run like everyone else?

I predicted Mike would reject me. I had revealed my story only once before to someone I was dating at that time but with disastrous results. It wasn't relevant to that person that I had been a child while a knife was held to my throat. He felt that I should have been strong, said no and not let it happen. At that time, I didn't get any further in telling my story and now I dreaded having to try again, convinced I would get the same reaction. But if we were ever to marry, then I owed it to Mike to tell him. It was my baggage and it went along for the ride with me everywhere.

I didn't plan to tell Mike when I did, but when I least expected it I lost control of keeping it in. We were fooling around in his room and getting ready to make love and he was being silly. He was taking off his shirt and the next thing I knew I saw his belt fly through the air. He had whipped it off in good fun and with a flourish, but the way he did it brought back a major flashback to that time I had been hit by

Nick's belt, and I ended up cowering at his feet. All the trust I had for Mike came crashing down in the heat of a fun-loving moment. As soon as I became aware of my reaction, I knew the charade was over. I wanted to curl into a ball, retreat deep within myself and never come out. But I couldn't, not this time.

Mike was quiet. He didn't say much. He let me ramble on and on. It was the first time I was ever permitted to keep going. I kept talking, the words spilling out, often incoherently, waiting for him to stop me. Waiting for his eyes to move away from me in disgust. Expecting him to let go of my hand, to pull away, repulsed. But he didn't let go and looked levelly at me from the chair he was sitting on and listened. It was the first healthy relationship I had experienced, so as he let me talk I let down my guard and told him everything. When I finished he calmly advised me to go to the police and seek counseling.

I took his advice and called the police who quickly turned me away, saying the statute of limitations was over for rape. Sadly, these officials did not recognize signs of trafficking, nor enquire if I had been a minor during the exploitation. Next, I went to the Rape Crisis Center on campus and told my story to a stranger. Shocked into silence, the stunned professional was unprepared for my story. It was a reaction I've faced many times since. The counselor recommended a group session for rape victims. I went along and one by one, each woman in the group shared their stories. Then it was my turn. All eyes fell upon me, the new girl. How could I describe in one to two sentences, and in less than two minutes, what had happened to me? I hadn't even processed the horror myself, nor received enough positive, supportive reactions to my story.

I simply couldn't share. I stood and walked out, never to return. My story didn't fit the parameters. Yes, I was raped. Yes, I was gang raped, attacked and left for dead. But that was only part of my story. That merely scratched the surface. It wasn't once, wasn't twice, but lasted for years, against my will and to pay back a debt for the benefit and profit of others. I was still lost in terms of wider support but Mike's help was so important to me.

Mike and I dated for the entire two years I attended college there and celebrated our graduation with our parents at a joint dinner. After college, Mike didn't ask me to marry him. He later told me that he didn't ask me because he thought I didn't want to get married because I was going to go to graduate school. I then confessed to him that I only went to graduate school because he hadn't asked me to marry him. At the time we had said we would part so we could both follow our individual dreams. Despite this perhaps sad miscommunication it was healing to know we didn't walk away from each other because of my past. The day I told Mike my story, he helped me begin the healing process. He accepted my past as history and loved the person I now was.

Mike encouraged me to take the first step to bring the men who did this to justice, to ask for help and get counseling. He gave me courage to accept myself and pursue my dreams. That day, Mike empowered me and I found my strength. The simple act of telling my entire story, being accepted without judgment, helped me survive and heal. Too many survivors, of any travesty, are not allowed this simple gift of sharing their tale to a compassionate, accepting and listening ear.

When I asked Mike to write a chapter for the book, I wondered what his perspective would be of the time I confessed my past to him, and what he had seen in my behavior and actions during those college years. We were from different worlds. An only child, Mike was raised by a single mum who worked hard as a secretary. They had a comfortable life, but there were times when it wasn't easy. He was just as astonished by my family background as I was by his. But regardless of our differences, he never questioned my past, never judged me, never expected me to be healed and get over it.

When Mike didn't propose to me I attended graduate school in a different state for a year and then worked as a waitress. Jim was somewhere in Florida in the Air Force and although we talked once in a while, things just never worked out for us to get together. I felt as if no one wanted me or would ever want the damaged me. I met a guy I worked with who was suave and fun to be around. We had the same family values, the same religion and felt we both wanted the same out of life. After dating for three months we decided we would be a good match and went ring shopping together. He never even proposed properly and we were married six months later. All my fairy-tale book ideas and dreams had been washed away with the years of abuse. I thought that this was the best I would ever get. I couldn't expect more. Deep down I felt lucky to have found someone to take me at all!

Just before my dad walked me down the aisle, he didn't say the normal things a father says to his little girl on her wedding day. He turned to me and said, 'Are you sure? You don't have to do this.'

I only shrugged and responded, 'It's OK.'

But I knew in my heart that it was too late to cancel it. Everyone was in their seats and the church was full and the music was playing the wedding march. Once again, I ignored all the red flags and warning bells in my head. I thought I would make the best of it. But the day after the wedding I started to see the reality of what I had done. The marriage wasn't consummated for a week. He wouldn't have sex when he thought I wanted it. He would only do it when he wanted it. He told me it was because it was a turn-off to him if I pursued it, even though we were married. I had absolutely no say in the matter. I soon learned that when it came to sex, with him it was really all about power.

When we returned home from the honeymoon, he sat me down at the kitchen table and told me, 'This is not a partnership. This is not fifty-fifty. I am the boss.'

I knew I was in trouble at that moment and that I had made a grave mistake. It was an emotionally and verbally abusive marriage that lasted for ten years. Even though I always worked full-time while we were together, I never had any money because he controlled my paycheck. I had to get money from him each week for approved purchases and wore the same clothes I had at college. All the while he enjoyed his import beers, and bought Ray-Ban sunglasses and designer clothes with our money.

My abandonment issues were so huge that when, after three years of marriage, my husband told me he was going to divorce me, I tried to kill myself. Looking back now, his threat of divorce was his way of keeping me 'in line' and controlling me because he knew I was extremely opposed to the idea of divorce and no one in my family had ever been divorced. It would have brought great shame upon the family and myself that I couldn't even have made this work.

The afternoon he told me he was leaving me, I had a meltdown. I went into a fetal position on the bathroom floor of our apartment as he walked out the door for work, leaving me with our two-year-old daughter looking down at me and rubbing my head. It was the first time I tried to commit suicide. Even though I was stuck in an abusive marriage, and only twenty-seven years old, the sheer thought of being left alone, abandoned and a failure of a wife was too much for me to handle. I broke. It was the accumulation of the sum of years of unspoken trauma.

I turned to the only people who I knew would never turn their back on me: my brothers. In fact, it was my baby brother Michael who rescued me that day. He was only twenty-one years old at the time. I called him to say goodbye and he rushed over and called an ambulance as well as my parents who didn't live far away. It's odd that I didn't call them. Perhaps I felt that I would be disappointing them. Michael took care of his two-year-old niece that day, as well as me. Our normal roles were reversed, as it was I who took care of him as we were growing up.

My husband decided to make another go of things

after that. When I was pregnant with our first child we had made plans to go overseas to visit his family at Christmas. My husband was the only one of his family living in the US and no one had been able to attend the wedding from his side. But I developed complications and was hospitalized and as the date neared for us to leave and I was released his father, a physician, advised us not to go abroad in case I had more medical problems. We agreed with his advice and stayed at home. Just after New Year's Day 1991, we got a call in the middle of the night. His brother had just been killed in a plane crash. 'This is all your fault. It's because of you that he died!' my husband screamed at me. 'If we had been there, then he wouldn't have died!' He blamed me. I was stunned.

He left for the funeral and stayed there for several months while I grew bigger and bigger. He called occasionally to inform me that he didn't know if or when he would return. Eventually, though, his parents made him come back to his expecting wife, but he continued to blame me for his brother's death.

Even after his abandonment of me during my first pregnancy, and the suicide attempt two years later, I stayed with him. We had another two children. But after ten years of his excessive drinking, taking care of three children mostly by myself while working full-time, his control over all the finances and his numerous affairs, I had had enough.

He had gotten a new job a few hours away and we had bought a house there. He was working at the new job during the week and coming home on the weekends. His mum was staying with us for a few months to help out. As much as I loved her, she was yet another responsibility for me. I had been packing all week and the removals men came one Saturday morning. My husband said he needed to go run a few errands early. I begged him to be quick because I was left there to supervise the men who were being paid hourly, as well as watching the kids and my mother-in-law who didn't speak English.

The day progressed to the afternoon and the men were almost finished loading up the van. I was exhausted and my husband was nowhere in sight. When the last box was loaded up, he came strolling in. 'Oh, good timing,' he declared happily. We loaded up the entire family in the Land Cruiser and drove four hours to our new house. We arrived around 2 a.m. at the new house and since the removals men were meeting us early the next day, we decided to camp out and sleep on the floor. The next day my husband said, 'I am going to take my mum and the kids to the hotel [where he had been staying during the week] so they aren't in the way and I will be right back.'

I am not sure why we didn't go there the night before for a good night's sleep in a bed and I was still seething from him not showing up the day before to help pack up the apartment.

'I need you to be back soon though because the men will be arriving at 9 a.m. and you have to pay them.'

I wasn't happy at all. The phones weren't set up yet and we didn't have mobiles. He just waved me off, leaving me all alone as he left with everyone. All morning I directed the men on where to put boxes and pieces of furniture as I unpacked. As it got later and later, I kept making excuses for him to the men. 'He should be here any time now!' I had no way of contacting him or the hotel. It was almost 4 p.m. when the last of the trucks was unloaded into the new house and I started to panic. Where was he? How was I going to pay them? I didn't have the checkbook. My hair was stuck to my head from the sweat and I was dirty from not having had a shower and unloading a three-bedroom house. I was physically and emotionally a mess.

Just as the last box was carried into the house, my husband strolled in and a feeling of déjà vu came over me. He was showered, wearing nicely pressed dress slacks and a fresh shirt and had a big smile on his face as he disregarded me. 'Hey guys. Great job. How about a cold beer?' He offered them the six-pack he was carrying in to the house. He looked at me and said, 'You look horrible. And you smell. Go take a shower. I am taking everyone out to dinner tonight.'

That was the last straw. I was thirty-five years old and felt as if I was sixty. All the years of abuse in my life came crashing down on me and I felt as if I had lived a very, very long time. For the first time in my life, I truly knew in my heart that I deserved more. And my children deserved more. I didn't know if I would ever get my knight in shining armor to save me, but it couldn't get any worse than the cards I had been dealt in life so far. I was going to have to be my own savior. The next morning I called a divorce attorney and started planning another escape.

Within months I had filed the divorce paperwork and one day I snuck out of our house with my three children. I took their clothing and toys, the photo albums of their lives and my journals. It was a vicious custody and divorce battle, but one I was determined to win for my freedom, physically as well as mentally.

Shortly after this, I reconnected with my first love, Jim. Long past being boyfriend and girlfriend, we rekindled our friendship. He and I had spoken occasionally throughout the years but had gone our separate ways. I always had a special place in my heart for him, and wondered what would have happened if we had married, but I knew that that wasn't meant to be for us. During all that time we never spoke of the day he had left my school. But I knew, even years later, that it would kill him to hear the truth of what I had endured. I knew he wouldn't be able to handle it. Nor did I have the courage to ask him what had happened to him in the school bathroom. But while we reminisced one day, the subject of the day he visited my school came up in conversation. It felt like the right time to tell my story.

But when I started to tell him, he quickly interrupted. 'I don't want to know,' he said gently.

'You don't?'

'I know something terrible happened back then, but I don't want to remember you differently.' He paused. 'Let's just leave it be. So my memory of you stays the same.'

A part of me was relieved that I didn't have to tell him and hurt him. Another part of me felt resentful that he was unable to hear it because it was too hard for him, while I had been forced to live through it, day after day for two years. We brushed it under the rug, silently agreeing never to discuss it. Nor did I tell him of the price I paid for leaning on him to be my protector. I'd never tried to find a protector after that happened. Jim died several years ago. He never knew.

I remember feeling very strongly at this time that it seemed like every time I trusted a man, they hurt or left me. Daniel, Jim, guys I tried to convince to help me, my ex-husband. And when I needed a man, they abandoned me. Scott wouldn't get involved, Jimmy left me at school and my dad never did anything to save me from the abuse of my husband. No one ever helped me.

It felt that I was truly all by myself.

15

Survivor

It would be many years later before I attempted to tell my story to anyone but Mike. The second time I spoke about it was to a female friend I worked with, Natalie. We were both single mums with three children each and struggling financially and emotionally. I knew she had been abused growing up and we both tried hard to be good mums, even though we had similar 'baggage' we were trying to heal from. We found support in each other and picked up the pieces when one of us was falling apart. I made sure her kids had Easter baskets when she was working so much overtime that she forgot the holiday. She picked up my little boy and took care of him when he was sick and I didn't have any leave from work and we kept a twenty-dollar bill at each of our houses in case one of us had an emergency. It was the closest friendship I had ever had.

I had tried to push Natalie away many times by not talking to her for months because of my trust issues. But I never seemed to be able to get rid of her. She was a friend for life and I wasn't used to that. So I decided I would tell her about my past, convinced it would send her running. But it didn't. She cried with me and now we work side-by-side educating others on why, many times, people stay in abusive situations and sometimes won't accept help.

Over the years I had attempted to tell my story but was rejected each time I started to tell it, stopping after only a few sentences. Shut down and turned away for trying to talk about something that made up who I was. Each rejection was devastating. Each time I retreated deeper inside myself, wounded in another way. Many a counselor sitting across from me would have a look of horror; others would be shocked and start to weep after hearing what I had physically endured. Each time this happened I got up and walked out, never to return.

Denial is a balm. People don't want to believe this happens in America, let alone in our communities. They may have heard of trafficking in other parts of the world or perhaps within the States, but that happens to girls who have been tricked and brought here from other countries like Russia and Mexico. People don't want to admit there is even a slim possibility that young American girls can be forced into prostitution or be exploited, especially not girls from the suburbs. Many believe suburban America is the safest place to raise their family. Not all the time.

Horrified by our stories, these people turn us away, unwilling to hear the nasty details. It is too close to home. By rejecting my story people are essentially saying that it is untrue. They don't just reject me but other girls like me. Their choice to react this way forces us to remain victims. Other trafficking survivors tell me of similar experiences. Too many counselors, who haven't been trained in this field, are uneducated about human trafficking and can't help us to heal. They don't know what to recommend.

So we endure alone. Many times, we self-medicate and barely survive each day. We secretly desire a fulfilling life where our nightmares no longer affect every aspect of our lives, but often it seems too much to hope for. Healing begins when we put a voice to our pain and tell the story of what happened to us. Too many women who have gone through various forms of trafficking tell me that they can't fathom telling people about what happened to them. They can't tell their story publicly. They can't form the words; even writing it down is too painful. The raw anguish eats away at them.

Telling my story makes me relive it. It brings the buried memories to the surface, making me feel vulnerable again. But I have chosen to do this. It is a vital component in moving from being a victim to a survivor. When I use my painful experience to help others, when I enter worthy relationships and learn to trust other people, I move from survivor to victorious thriver. The abuse is only part of my story, part of my life. When another person accepts my story, and all of me, it helps me to accept myself. Then I move from not merely surviving each day to beginning to thrive.

Twenty-four years after the abuse ended, I sought out a therapist who could help me heal. A counselor had said, 'It's not *if* you need a therapist, but when.' For me, I needed help from someone trained in what I had experienced. I had gone to a few rape crisis centers, but I did not fit their typical rape client profile. One counselor asked if she could hypnotize me. There were so many details I couldn't remember because of the many times I had passed out or was so shocked I couldn't recall what had exactly happened. Nightmares haunted me night after night. I wanted to know, yet was afraid to know. Could I release the control I had constructed over my mind and surrender to the unknown? I was afraid of what my mind would do when I finally uncovered what was carefully buried. Would I have a nervous breakdown? Would I go crazy? The nightmares were bad enough but what demons would be released if I remembered all the details?

After hearing part of my story, another counselor didn't want to hear anymore. She advised me to leave the details buried. 'Why bother to dig them up?' She recommended that I store the bad memories away in a box in my mind. Fill the box with the ordeal, close the lid and lock it. I didn't understand this but it was the only advice I had received. I hoped I would be able to sleep better but was frightened that one day the box would be suddenly opened. But locking the memories away in a Pandora's Box had the same result as in the myth. I needed to write this book, but I was afraid to open the box. Would I ruin all the hard work I had done over the years to heal? Would revealing these memories catapult me into a nervous breakdown? Or would I remain strong and capable, able to deal with the horrific memories of my past? Had I healed enough?

This was the turning point for me. If I truly was healed then I could endure the writing of this book. As an approach to further healing, I began to write bits and pieces for myself. The blank, receptive paper was a safe place to release the nightmares that plagued my mind.

As my oldest daughter neared the age that I was when my abuse had begun, I realized that I needed to write this for others, for parents and professionals. I wanted to wake our community up to the danger of not standing up for another when we know something is wrong. It is not enough to leave it to the police. Things are not always as they appear. For those who have endured their own traumatic experiences, I want to empower them, to remind them they do have options.

Writing my story was hard work. Night after night I wrote, taking long breaks to recover. My initial motive was not to publish but to process. Going public meant revealing my carefully concealed humiliation. Several people agreed my slavery was a terrible thing for a child to live through, but it would be best if I kept quiet. 'You'll risk your safety and the safety of your children,' they cautioned. 'You'll risk your reputation,' added another. 'You will look bad.' The irony of the last statement still surprises me. Why is my reputation spoiled because of what evil men did to me? 'Putting this horrible abuse out in public is selfish,' someone said.

One night, a person I had just started dating confronted me about it. 'I don't think you should publish this. If you do, I won't be able to date you.'

Confused, I asked him why.

'I have a very important position at work and go to many high-powered dinners and fundraisers. I can't have you on my arm next to me with people knowing this.'

263

I was stunned into silence. When I recovered, I replied, 'Then there's the door.' I've never regretted the decision. Although I was saddened by his opinion that this would make me a less desirable date or future wife, it also empowered me to accept my path and move forward. I knew I was gaining strength daily and healing by the minute.

During the years after my divorce, when I was trying to heal, I spent a lot of time at local bookstores searching through the aisles of self-help books. I spent a great deal of money on anything I could get my hands on that might help, listened to CDs in my car and completed numerous workbooks which promised to make me normal again. Each one had its own truth that I drew upon. And I knew deep in my heart that each book I held in my hand had been destined to be there, at the exact time that I needed what was inside it to help me on the next phase of my recovery.

As I grew closer to the core of the problem, I realized that I needed to embrace the truth. Yes, I was frightened to tell others. Yes, I was scared that I might be found again by my abusers. Yes, I was scared that my children would be hurt. But the more research I did, the more people I talked to, the more I was convinced that this was my life's mission. I needed to turn this unspeakable evil into something good.

A wall at the National Underground Railroad

Freedom Center in Cincinnati reads: 'If not now, then when?' I had dreamed, wished and prayed for a person to help me, for someone to believe me, to help me and for God to send someone to rescue me. That person never showed up. Not the guidance counselor who failed to ask why my grades were falling, the principal who didn't ask why I had skipped class, the security guard in the school hallway who ignored the physical abuse I endured, the teachers who turned their back when I was being harassed, the cop who took me home after being kidnapped, drugged, and left for dead, my boyfriend who knew something was amiss, fellow students who knew I was being bullied. No one took the harder path.

I have no doubt that when the people who knew me when I was teenager read this, they will be shocked and stunned. Perhaps I should have gone into acting rather than social work. My survival depended on my ability to act as if everything was normal, to keep the abusers' secret and mine. As well as suffering tremendous abuse, I also did my chores, went out with friends, participated in family vacations, worked at my part-time job and had a long-distance boyfriend.

But how does someone begin to ask the right questions? Would I have answered truthfully? The policeman knew something of my situation, but I was too frightened to confide in him. Would anyone have believed me if I'd told my secret? Even now, it seems unbelievable that a girl in an upper-class suburb in the United States was trafficked. I thought I had good self-esteem. I had good parents who provided well for me. But people prey on others. Their practiced eye saw my weakness. I was an outsider, new in the area, and I craved more attention at home. I cared too much about what others thought of me. I felt I was responsible for the well-being of my family. At the end of the day, I did what I felt I had to do to protect myself and my family. I was willing to endure the torture so that my parents didn't get the wrong impression of me, that they didn't believe something that wasn't true, so that my brothers and pet wouldn't get hurt. I couldn't handle that. It was easier to endure what I had to than see them get hurt.

Some say I was stupid. I should never have fallen for their threats. Vulnerable, my soul broken after the rape, they circled in for the attack like hungry sharks who smelt blood. How was it possible that people were unaware that a sweet, young child from the suburbs was being sexually exploited?

The important thing to accept is that I felt I couldn't tell anyone. I was terrified of the consequences. I believed I had no options. No choices. No free will. That is why it is called slavery. I was brainwashed, convinced that no one would believe my story if I told them it. Reduced to nothing inside, I was sure that the welfare of my beloved family rested solely on my behavior. I was without hope, happiness, or a future. I was left only with shame.

As I have shared my story, people have often insisted that I must have had a choice. 'You could have walked away at any time, told your parents or a teacher,' they say. Did I have a choice? Perhaps I did. But as a terrified child, physically hurt and threatened, I didn't feel that I had a choice. And that is all that really matters. Perhaps the choice I made was to go through with it, naively believing it would be only one time. I planned to return the first time with the photos in my hands. I was not prepared for the depth of evil these men were capable of, nor did I imagine people would be mercilessly abusive to a young girl.

Additionally, I felt the safety of my family, and the security of my father's job, was mine to protect. I planned to keep my reputation and my pride intact. Instead, I was damaged physically and emotionally.

'How did you survive?' That is the first question I am asked when I tell my story at speaking engagements. People wonder how I could go to college, get married and raise children after what I had endured. God provided a way and gave me the strength to get through my ordeal. The fact that I am here now to help save others is a miracle. Statistically, I should be dead, in jail, have committed suicide, become a drug addict or severely dysfunctional due to my past.

Since escaping the bondage and doing deep work with a good therapist, I can see that the post-traumatic stress disorder I suffered actually helped me survive. Trauma victims frequently use disassociation. They compartmentalize their lives in order to survive day to day. I recognized very early on that to go on, I had to shove the pain away and become as emotionally detached as possible. If I wanted to make love to my husband, I had to bury those nightmares. If I didn't do this, I might not be able to function at all. And if I couldn't function then my captors would have won, again. I knew it wasn't healthy – I wasn't really dealing with the issue – but this coping method allowed me to survive.

Lying in the bathtub one night, I knew it was time, time to pour out the past onto paper. As I pondered this thought, I wondered what would happen not if, but when I finally opened Pandora's Box and wrote my story for others to read. This bath was different from the other baths. It was a turning point. Even though I would expose my naked self, my soul, I would finally be whole. Finally be cleansed and washed free of these years of sin and guilt, of the secrets and the what-ifs.

Baths have always been a symbolic experience for me, almost spiritual. Most women enjoy baths. They soak in the warm, sudsy, scented waters, soaking away the craziness of the day, the responsibilities and chaos. Baths give you permission to unwind. They are relaxing, peaceful, tranquil and medicinal. But they also represent something much more than relaxing or cleansing our bodies. Our first breath is taken as we emerge from the uterine bag of water in which we developed and lived for our first months of existence. Next we are washed clean and presented to our parents, to the world. Parents document their child's first bath as momentous. Many of us receive the waters of baptism to symbolically cleanse us of sin, proclaiming our commitment to be followers of Christ. At death, many receive final rites, a blessing of holy water by a priest. Baths and water not only cleanse us but also mark important events in our lives. They cleanse our souls and make us new again. They heal us and nourish our souls. Our body requires water in order to survive.

Taking a bath has always been important to me. Baths allowed me to think deeply and have a good cry, which no one could hear while the hot water gushed from the faucet. Baths permitted me an opportunity for soul-searching and at times provided me with answers to my questions. But I also took baths for another important reason. They were taken with an earnest wish of washing away sins and regrets – my regrets and the sins of others. But this never seemed to happen. Baths were taken as a cleansing ritual, to start a new beginning, a rebirth with fresh, clean water. Yet the dirty feeling still remained after exiting the waters.

For all these years, I have carried the burden of what happened to me and that memorable bath when all this started when I was fifteen years old. Many times I've reflected on this dark part of my life. This ordeal lasted for a period of time that I cannot wholly bring my broken memory to recall, I suppose for protection of my fragile mind. The one thing I vividly recall is the empty feeling I had each day. I went through the motions and the facade of growing up a normal teenager during these years while privately enduring hell on earth.

The night I decided to put my experience on to paper, the fragrant, warm water embraced and soothed me like a soft womb. After long years locked within the dark corners of my mind, the memories slowly seeped out. I had kept them contained, afraid that if I allowed myself to remember, my fragile state of mind might crack.

I pride myself on being a strong woman. I had endured more than most people could ever fathom. After all, I had survived my own nightmare, hadn't I? But that was physical. This was mental. One can never guarantee how strong the psyche really is. Or what the results will be. Was I strong enough now? Had I healed enough to go down this path? To remember what I had endured? To press myself to remember the parts I had blocked to protect myself? Could I face the silent horrors that no one knew about?

The ability to reason and find solutions is limited in an immature young teen. What kid is equipped to deal with such adult horrors? How was I supposed to know what to do in such an overwhelming and dangerous situation? What kid makes a decision to be exploited? To be raped over and over again? To stay awake all night long, locked away in a stranger's room, being hurt and violated in secret by multiple men? I believe a few people did know something was happening. The teachers and employees of the high school which I attended and the mothers whose houses I visited late each night. The teachers never questioned the times they saw me pulled out of class by the older Chaldeans. They allowed me to go as if I'd simply asked for a hall pass to use the restroom. Yet they were adults and I was a child. By doing nothing, turning a blind eye, they allowed themselves to be controlled by this gang and permitted a child in their care to be hurt in ways they could never have imagined.

I dreamed that one day my typing teacher, math teacher, study hall monitor, the teacher whose class was near my locker, or the security guard would say, 'Theresa, can I help you? Are you being threatened?

Are they hurting you? Do you need to talk?' Unlike an inner city school with metal detectors, this was a ritzy, high-class school, where most students' fathers made lots of money. I do not blame my parents for being oblivious. But I do blame the teachers and trained school personnel who never offered to help when they observed a kid clearly being manipulated. They saw me slammed against the locker, spat on, and harassed. Almost daily, they watched me leave with the Chaldeans.

Frequently away from campus during normal school hours I never received a detention or got reprimanded for skipping class. Unlike the kid who left early to go and party after school, my eyes were dull, my head was down, and I never smiled. I was the picture of dread, flanked by two Chaldean cousins as I passed the teacher in the hall. My constant challenge was what lie I would tell my mother to explain why I wasn't home right after school. Teenagers create excuses to get out of school assignments and chores to spend time with friends. I lied to protect my family. To stay alive. I was good at it because the stakes were so high.

Instead of attending the four or five track practices held each week, I often made it to only one. I told the coach I had a job and couldn't always be there. At the same time, I'd tell my mum I was at track practice. Though I lived within walking distance of the school, my mother didn't come to see me practice. Nor did the coach call my parents to verify that I had a job. As long as I had a qualifying speed, I was permitted to compete in the track competitions. I only competed in home events, and I only recall my mum attending one event. Easy enough to lie to them then.

Babysitting after school was another excuse. No one asked for the phone number where I was, or asked to see the money I made. In reality, I was working all right, but making money for someone else. The cousins frequently came into the fast-food place where I worked, just to let me know they were there, keeping an eye on me. They called the restaurant phone number and asked for me. I got in trouble for personal calls at work, and when I answered, they didn't say a word. But they never took me from work or even directly afterwards. That was traceable. They knew my parents or the police could track what time I left. The physical abuse left marks and bruises. 'Oh, that bruise?' I would say casually. 'I got that from not making it over the hurdle at track practice. Boy, did that hurt.' 'My brother hit me,' I'd explain away another mark. Or, 'I ran into something at work.'

Being new to the area, no one knew how I acted or performed in school before moving there. No one saw the changes in my behavior. That is one of the things that made me vulnerable to the exploitation.

I had no support system. No accountability. No extended family to notice changes. In those parts of town, neighbors minded their own business, refusing to interfere or pry unless something directly affected them. The only ones who had a strong inkling were my brothers. But being children and younger than me they were struggling with their own difficulties.

Internal physical pain was put down to monthly menstruation pain or, as my mum termed it, growing pains. I experienced a lot of growing pains in those days. The guys were usually careful not to hit me in the face. The times Nick backhanded me, I covered the bruise with make-up. Marks on other parts of my body were hidden under clothing. If it is hot and a woman wears long sleeves, it is a pretty good indicator that she is hiding something. When my hair was nearly pulled out to keep me still, the small bald spots were hidden under a hat or a different hairstyle. When my legs were torn apart to restrain me, the sore joints and muscles were invisible. Invisible like the internal memories.

Children will naturally do anything to please their parents to stay in their good graces and make them proud. Children experiencing sexual or physical abuse go to great lengths to try to please their parents. My father held a powerful position, one that meant everything to him. His company had salesmen all over the world. At the annual awards ceremony, only three were honored with the highest award of a gold ring and a trip. My father received that award twice. The second year, an emerald chip was added to his ring.

My dad traveled weekly, leaving mum to raise the four of us alone. She was the single parent of the 1980s. Although she never had to worry about money, she was lonely. Eventually she mingled with others and found her own interests outside of the family. In addition to my family's own personal challenges, my dad was frequently required to entertain customers. Ironic that I was doing the same thing in an underground way for someone else's business. Dad took customers out to dinner, followed by drinks late into the night. My mum was usually home with us kids, but at least once a week my parents dressed up and went out together.

Beautiful with her blond hair, blue eyes, and shining smile, my mum glowed as she prepared for the evening, excited my dad was home and happy for a night out without the kids. We knew they wouldn't be home until the early morning hours. As one of my brothers described, 'They led their own lives, and we were along for the ride.' Baggage I suppose. They loved us, but were distracted by climbing the social ladder, maintaining the big house in the right neighborhood, two cars, and yearly camping vacations.

My siblings believed we did an inordinate amount of

chores compared to most kids. At least it seemed like it to us. My parents were not affectionate or emotionally attached. They were functional parents who believed in family and a strong work ethic. It was all part of the equation that added up to a good kid from the suburbs being exploited by gang members. Most people didn't realize, but there were those who suspected something and chose not to do anything about it.

Right or wrong, it is what it is. I cannot change it. I am the woman I am today because I met the devil and lived in hell. Having experienced both the dark and the light, I prefer to live in the light. I choose to use my past as a stepping stone to something good. I choose not to be quiet. I want to help save another young girl from being tied up and taken against her will until she loses consciousness, in order to give meaning to the pain I endured, the lies I had to tell, and the invisible marks I suffered.

I believe my soul wasn't with me during the time of abuse; it retreated into a protection mode. This saved my life and my sanity. Had my soul stayed and endured the years of torture, I would have been a broken person forever. I could have given in, turned my back on my family and remained a sex slave, a full-time prostitute for the Chaldean ringleader's benefit. Until they wearied of me that is and replaced me with a younger, fresher girl and disposed of me physically or threw me aside with nowhere to go.

I could have ended up in a mental institution, driven crazy from the abuse, with no one to confide in. Though I felt empty, my body devoid of a soul, I also felt a protective bubble encircling me, an energy that appeared when I was alone with my thoughts and my despair, showering me with love, giving me strength to endure the ordeal until it was finished. I believe this energy was made up of my angels, cleansing away any harm that had been done each day, repairing the physical, mental, and spiritual damage. Making my body whole again, even without my soul. This energy, these angels, kept me alive. Kept me going so that I could be rejoined with my soul later and begin the healing process, have a family and someday tell my story. This process allowed me to help others who endured horrors from which their souls temporarily retreated as well.

I felt the angels' presence but didn't realize what they had done for me until much later. Unable to find a therapist equipped to handle my story, I was doing self-therapy through journaling when I suddenly became very angry. 'How could you let this happen to me?' I demanded of God. 'Where were you when I needed you? All those times for years, as I lay there being abused over and over again?'

With calming clarity, I heard Him say to me, 'I was right there with you, Theresa, making sure that nothing worse happened. You could have died! You endured what I knew you could handle. When it would have been more than you could bear, I stopped it.'

A wave of memories washed over me. Scene after scene, and in moments when I could no longer take another person climbing upon me there would be a knock at the door, ending the abuse. The times the knife held at my throat would suddenly drop from the man's hands. I could have been killed, left for dead in a strange, out-of-the-way place. The possibilities of being tortured beyond what had occurred flooded my mind.

I wondered how I didn't become pregnant after all the times I was forced to have unprotected sex with dozens, hundreds, thousands of men. Why hadn't I thought of this before? I never used any protection and certainly none of the men cared enough for me or their possible children to use a condom. I was never a human being to them. I should have been plagued with sexually transmitted diseases. Based on the number of men who obviously were not careful with their own sexual health, my chances of being passed an incurable disease was nearly impossible to miss. Yet the only complication I experienced was the human papilloma virus (HPV).

'My angels surrounded you during the baths,' the Lord lovingly explained. 'They washed away the harm your body received. Cleansing, healing you from the inside out.'

Dr Jeffery Barrows, an OB/Gyn who lectures to physicians about the medical implications of prostitution for women, offers a medical theory to explain why I didn't get pregnant. 'The body can stop ovulating during traumatic events,' he told me. 'It is possible that this is what your body did the entire two years. Emotional stress has a vast influence on the reproductive system. Severe life-threatening stress would likely cause you to stop ovulating on a regular basis. The process of ovulation is very intricate and very much under the control of the central nervous system. When a woman is not ovulating, she will not get pregnant. This likely scenario is supported by the fact that you reported to me that during this difficult season in your life, you experienced long episodes when you did not have a period, and when they occurred, they were very irregular. This is typical for a woman who is not ovulating on a regular basis. Therefore it is quite easy to attribute the fact that you did not get pregnant through this time of repeated forced sexual activity to the secondary emotional stress that was brought on by this terrible ordeal.'

I believe in miracles. While this can be explained medically, I firmly believe that God knew the limits of what I could endure. He had a greater plan for my life.

16
Reaching out

I started my charity Traffickfree because I believed that some day we would have a world free of trafficking. Some might believe that this is a lofty dream but Martin Luther King Jr had a dream to see America as a country where people were not judged on the color of their skin, but on the content of their character. And Susan B. Anthony dreamed too of a country where women were free to vote and had equal rights.

I carefully chose a logo for Traffickfree that would represent my past. I chose red for the red flags that people need to be aware of when someone is being trafficked or exploited. The signs people ignored when it was happening to me. Angel Wings symbolize the angels who protected me during the time I was enslaved and for the angel who I met in the diner the night of my kidnapping and asked me the simplest question, 'Can I help you?' And I chose the heart, to signify God's love for me and a reminder to love myself first.

Even when I started sharing my story publicly, I still thought I was the only one with a story where someone lived at home, but was being trafficked by someone from her school and at night while sneaking out. But I was wrong. 'Thank you for sharing. My story's just like yours,' a fifty-year-old woman with graying hair whispered into my ear as she gave me a huge bear hug after one of my presentations. 'I have never told anyone,' one email began. 'I heard you speak and I never knew what happened to me was called this. Thank you,' yet another email read. 'I have been free for thirty-five years …' an anonymous note read that appeared in my mail box.

Emails and letters started to pour in. There were those from a young college student in her early twenties who had been sold by her mum when she was four years old. I would get her emails in the morning when I woke up, noticing that they had been sent at 2 or 3 a.m., probably written and delivered when she couldn't sleep. 'I know counselors can help a lot, but it's not the same as someone who understands your pain,' she wrote. She just needed someone who had been there before too. Someone she didn't have to explain how she was feeling to and what was going through her mind. She had been traumatized sexually, had PTSD and Stockholm syndrome, but no health insurance though she needed major counseling from a qualified person who knew this issue. She just needed an understanding person to listen to her. Someone to tell her she wasn't crazy.

The list goes on and on. I keep every card and email on a bulletin board hanging on my wall as a daily reminder of why I am doing this. For all the other Theresas out there.

Once I learned the name of what had happened to me, I set out to read everything I could get my hands on about trafficking. I attended conferences, watched movies and talked to experts. I was determined to be more than just a survivor with a story. I didn't realize it then but I was preparing myself for the next part of my journey, as a thriver by becoming an expert.

Soon it wasn't enough to fly thousands of miles to be given five minutes on stage to share my story and make people cry so they would contribute to a fundraiser for a trafficking organization. I wanted more. I wanted to teach people *why* this happens, *how* you would know it, and what is going on all around us that is making us numb to immorality and sex. So much so that sex addictions are rampant, pornography sites on the Internet exceed 200 million pages and apathy and acceptance have allowed inappropriate television shows and magazines to become what we once thought of as pornographic but now are 'just the way it is'.

Throughout my travels, all across the world, I have been blessed to speak to many groups of people. People who are curious, anxious to learn and even those who are apprehensive about coming but were dragged to the event by their spouse or friend. It hasn't been easy. I left my full-time social work job and a steady paycheck to speak out about human trafficking in 2008 after I used up all my vacation time to speak at events. I needed to make a life-changing decision. It was scary to know I had three children to support and bills to pay. Leaving my job would mean I wouldn't have the security of a paycheck, and needed to find other ways to support them, keep the lights on and food in the refrigerator. But I knew I needed to do it.

I have missed my children's baseball games, soccer games and school meetings because I was somewhere far from home telling people about my experience of being a sex slave. I was stranded in an airport while my daughter was in hospital. I have lived for five days with one set of clothing and no medication because my luggage was lost while traveling. I have spoken outdoors in parks with people walking by, out for a leisurely walk with no idea what they were going to be hearing that morning. I have done presentations in men's maximum-security prisons and had a prisoner ask me afterwards, 'Are you scared?' I thought about it carefully for a minute and I responded honestly, 'No. There isn't anything you can do to me that hasn't already been done!' He looked at me and smiled and said, 'Good' and walked away. I left the prison that day feeling more empowered than ever.

I have shared my story at 'John Schools' where men who have tried to buy a prostitute and were arrested now have to attend an all-day course to learn the realities of what they were doing, with hopes that it will deter them from doing it again. One day I talked to a room full of 'johns' who ranged in age from eighteen to eighty years old, of all different ethnicities, including one man with an interpreter and one man on an oxygen tank. After sharing my story with them, a 'john' asked me, 'I don't get it. Why didn't you just tell your parents?'

I became livid and said something I don't get the opportunity to tell normal audiences. 'What part of this did you not understand? The part where I said I was being threatened, beaten or raped?'

His response was still one of disbelief and judgment for my lack of actions. I then asked him, 'Sir, do you have a daughter?'

He said, 'Yes.'

And that was when I lowered the boom. 'And you were out paying to have sex with another person's daughter.'

I walked away that day feeling that even if I hadn't changed his mind or his behavior, at least I had stood up for myself.

Several weeks later, I received an email from the prosecuting attorney's office, who conduct the classes. He forwarded me a letter that he had received from the man I'd had the confrontation with and it said, 'I want to apologize for my actions on soliciting a woman and to Ms Flores as well. I know now what I did was wrong.' It was a victory for every victim out there.

Why is it that people's reaction to a victim's story is usually, 'Why didn't you just leave or tell someone?' Why isn't the question we are asking, 'How could a man do this to a girl or woman?' or 'Why don't we have stronger laws against this atrocity?' or 'What drives a man to degrade women, to become a pimp or pay for sex?' Those are the only questions we should be asking.

I have found that doing television interviews has been more difficult than speaking to a large group of people. You have a shorter period of time, and then they edit it down to two or three minutes, take out the important things and leave only the parts that serve for shock value and ratings. However, I realize that by doing a TV interview or going on a show means I can reach a far greater number of people than I can at a presentation. My goal has always been to get this information out to as many people as possible. So doing interviews for TV has always been a double-edged sword for me.

I have had to do seven interviews in a row, before having to dash on stage for an hour presentation, having to tell my story once again. I did a TV interview in Denver in a janitor's closet because it was the only quiet space to go. It was difficult being in such a small, confined room and after sharing a snippet of my story and explaining why I was there that day, the female reporter looked at me with disbelief and asked, 'Really? Who were they? Do you know their names?'

I was shocked. Did she not just hear that I went to school with them? 'Of course I know their names,' I responded.

'Well what are they?' she demanded to know.

'If I tell you that, then I am dead,' I said as I took off the microphone and started to walk out of the closet.

The male cameraman came up to me after he had packed up the equipment in the van and said with sad but compassionate eyes, 'I am really sorry about that.

And I am sorry for what happened to you.'

I have done an interview on live TV that was broadcast internationally and online while the host, a grandfatherly man in his eighties, asked if the men trafficking me had 'put objects inside me' and told the viewers, 'They even tied her to the bed spread-eagled.' At that moment, I would have given anything to have had the courage to get off the tall stool and walk out. But I forced myself to stay put and used the opportunity to explain to him and the predominately Christian audience the reality of what victims regularly endure.

As I left the TV station that day, another thought occurred to me. Thank God it had been *me* sitting through that interview. It had been 30 years since I had lived that horror. I couldn't imagine if that interview had been with a younger survivor, perhaps in her twenties, having just escaped the same life. Most likely it would have done immense damage to her. I was glad it had been me instead.

Besides sharing my story through Traffickfree, I started to train law enforcement officers, judges, child service workers, social workers, high school and college students and church members. Basically anyone who wanted to know. But after every presentation, I noticed people's faces as they left the auditoriums. They were sad and you could sense the heaviness in their hearts as they walked out with their shoulders slumped and heads down. When they asked me what they could do to help stop this epidemic, I didn't have a good answer for them. I told them that they could write letters to politicians for stronger laws and to advertising companies to stop using explicit images of girls, also to boycott certain food manufacturers who don't sign fair trade agreements. But it didn't seem like enough. I realized they needed something to do about this specific issue and I asked myself, *but what could someone really do to help?*

And then one night, in a moment of panic, it came to me. I was driving home from a presentation in Detroit. It was the first time I had returned so close to my old home and I wasn't thrilled about it. But I knew I needed to do it to heal and for all the other girls being trafficked right then in Detroit. It was late at night when I left the hall, around 10 p.m., and it was cold, dreary and dark. As I drove home, facing a three-hour drive, I noticed the road signs weren't matching with my map. I had gotten lost. Then I started to see signs for the towns where the traffickers had taken me to be sold. Although it was twenty-seven years later, I freaked out. A flashback of the night I was kidnapped entered my mind with full force as I was trying to find my way out of Detroit.

At that moment I realized that I wasn't doing

enough. I could talk about what happened to me all day and night and yet it wasn't going to change the fact that there were girls out there, right that minute, possibly in a motel, living a nightmare and they had no idea what to do or how to escape. They don't know they are a 'human trafficking victim'. They don't know there are services for them. No one is asking them 'Can I help you?' And they don't know that there is a national human trafficking hotline phone number they can call to just talk to someone who understands and that can offer them another option.

And then it came to me: I needed to get them that phone number. That way they could call in their worst moment, no matter where that happened to be, when they were ready to talk and get out. As I found my way through the city of Detroit that night and got back on the right road, I decided I would put this number on the back of bars of soap used in motels, because every girl washes up after each man in an attempt to wash him off her. Wash away the memories of what just happened to her. Many times, it is also the only place she is permitted to go alone.

But how would I get the soaps into the motels? I decided to give it to them for free. ('You said the magic word! Free,' one motel manager told a team of volunteers delivering soap during an outreach.) I also wanted to add a few questions for the girls to read

289

so they would know why the hotline number was on there. *Are you being forced to do something you don't want to do?* My answer to that question would have been yes. *Have you been threatened if you try to leave?* Again, my answer would have been yes. And I felt it was important to have a question for the man buying her or for the person staying in the room down the hall who was seeing men come in and out of a room all night long.

Are you witnessing young girls being prostituted? People had seen me being used and exploited but had done nothing. Perhaps they hadn't known what to do.

I spent every day and night researching where to order the perfect-sized soap from, designing the labels and locating printers. I asked people to help me buy the soap and they did. I asked people to volunteer to put on the labels and they did. I went to the Super Bowl and asked people to come and take them out to motels and they did. And something amazing started to happen. The motels took the soap! We heard over and over again from motel managers and staff. I was shocked. This might just work!

As I drove back to Ohio from Texas after the very first outreach, the Super Bowl, I had a smile on my face and a check in my purse from a generous church that had donated enough money to pay back what I had borrowed to do the outreach. There had been a call put in an alternative newspaper in Dallas and the surrounding areas asking for 10,000 strippers to go there for the weekend to 'meet the demand'. And we had just distributed exactly 10,000 bars of soap with the national human trafficking hotline number on them to motels all around Dallas!

This was possible. This was something people could do. Senior citizens, kids, anyone could label a bar of soap. The phone started ringing and requests started to come in from churches and organizations wanting to help. People whose hearts had been touched by this issue and didn't know what to do about it or how to help. I kept hearing, 'Can I help you?'

The phone calls to Polaris Project in Washington DC, an organization that combats slavery throughout the world, doubled during our outreaches too. We started to do other sporting events and, over and over again, motel clerks pointed out pictures of missing and runaway children that they recognized from the posters we took out with the soap. They told us, 'Yes, I saw her here last week with an older man.'

And from that information the police were able to gain valuable leads and rescue them. People started to believe in a cause. They started to donate and felt as if they could make a difference. They could help a victim. One tiny bar of soap with a red sticker and a phone number could rescue a girl from being a sex slave. I decided to call it something as simple as the idea: S.O.A.P. (Save Our Adolescents from Prostitution).

But what it stood for wasn't simple. It was life-changing, for the volunteers, for me and for the girls being raped and beaten repeatedly, night after night.

I don't regret a single decision I have made. Would I have preferred to have followed a different path? Not accepted that ride home from school from a cute guy I had a crush on? Sure. Would I not have accepted that fizzy drink had I known it was drugged? Sure. Would I have decided to tell my mother what happened to me the day I was raped or confided in the policeman who rescued me after being left for dead in a motel? Sure. But I didn't. I can't change any of it. I can only go forward. I don't have time to worry about 'what if's', what could have been, and choose only to forgive. Because it is not up to me to be the judge of others' actions.

I know I will always be working on my healing, peeling the layers of the onion back a little at a time. Crying with each layer but knowing that through each layer of pain, comes the sweetness of moving on and that it gets easier with time.

Even though I have had some difficult experiences while sharing my story and doing this publicly, I wouldn't change it for the world. I have never felt more acceptance, more support, more love and validation in my entire life.

Helping others find their voice, and letting them know what name to give what happened to them, or by educating motels on the signs and giving them a phone number to call, or by mobilizing volunteers to give a girl a way out, has been all worth it. And I would do it all over again if just to save one girl from a life of being a sex slave.

A note from Patrick

I was the younger brother who followed my big sister everywhere. Almost two years apart in age, I wanted to be with my big sister every waking moment. 'Get me a drink of water,' she would say when she didn't want me around. She would send me on an errand to the kitchen. 'Get me a snack from the refrigerator.' I always obliged. I wanted to be important to her in the way she was to me.

When I was eight I showed Theresa I loved her by scaring her. To get a reaction from her I'd hide under her bed and hiss like a snake. She'd run screaming down the hall until she figured out it was just her pesky little brother. When she came back into the room, I'd take off running.

As we grew, we slowly drifted apart. She was a girl;

I was a boy. She liked to do girl things and I was into boy things. When we attended the same junior high school and high school, she gave me the talk. 'When we're at school, don't talk to me. I have my friends,' she said. Theresa had outgrown my stage of grossing her out with slime and squirting her with silly string but I had so looked forward to being at the same school as her.

By the time we moved to Birmingham, I had attended five elementary schools and two junior highs. I would go on to attend three more high schools and move across country in the middle of my senior year. But for now we were in Birmingham, probably for a couple years. Our folks promised the moving would stop but Dad's career was the focus of his life. I rarely saw him and when I did he'd be reading the newspaper or watching television with a drink in his hand. His job was stressful and a lot was expected of him so we, his family, picked up the slack. Still, we missed him at dinners and during weeklong business trips. He came from an era where the man's job was to provide for the family and the woman's job was to raise the kids.

Dad should've read the manual on Mum before he married her. Mum was not a woman to sit idly by just raising the kids. Growing up with one sister and six brothers, my mum had a zest for life and wanted to experience everything. Each move had challenges, but Mum supported her husband. Every place we lived, Mum made it an adventure. Any question we had, Mum answered it. She answered our questions about sex and relationships and made sure we could all cook. Mum called herself Mum and Dad. The older we got, the less time we spent as a family. Today we all live in different states, hundreds of miles from one another.

By the time we arrived in Birmingham, Mum was raising two teens and two boys aged eleven and nine. When we moved to Birmingham, all the fun and games stopped. A dark heaviness settled over our family. My parents attributed the dark mood to teenage hormones. In retrospect, I realize it was a spiritual darkness.

My first memory of interacting with the Chaldeans was when I was in eighth grade. A boy told me that if I didn't do what he said, he would have his cousins hurt my sister. 'Your sister is their property,' he said. I was shy and introverted and picked on incessantly. Even the nerds picked on me. But this one time, I fought back. This was about my sister. 'Bite me, dirt bag,' I said to the overweight boy antagonizing me.

'Your sister is gonna get it now,' he threatened.

That evening I mentioned what he'd said to Theresa. The color drained from her face.

The next day the overweight Chaldean apologized.

'I made it up,' he said. I knew he was lying.

By ninth grade I had racked up many encounters with Chaldeans, both at junior high and high school. The white kids stayed away from them. Teachers pretended not to see anything that involved a Chaldean.

There was an unwritten code everyone lived by, though I didn't understand why. For several months I was followed in the school halls and home from school by Chaldeans. Then, I took my first theater class and fell in love. I was meant for the stage. Soon it became the center of my life. The theater was also the one place where the Chaldeans didn't follow me.

Every once in a while, Theresa told me to take a different route while walking home from school. At first I figured she didn't want to be seen with me. But I saw how the Chaldean boys sneered at her. It made my skin crawl. The only one I liked was Daniel because I knew Theresa liked him. One day I was standing by the school bookstore and Daniel's sister came up to me. She was beautiful. 'Hi,' she said.

'Hi,' I answered shyly.

'You're cute.'

I was speechless, which made her smile. 'I like you,' she continued. 'So I'm going to tell you something. Be careful of my cousins.'

'Your cousins?'

'They're hurting your sister,' she confided. Suddenly

her sisters and female cousins moved around her like the Secret Service guarding the president.

'The cousins will not like you talking to a white boy,' one said.

The male cousins clustered behind me, hemming me in. They began shouting in their language. 'Why is it OK for you to be with white girls,' Daniel's sister shouted defiantly, 'but we cannot like white boys?'

'You should not say such things,' one of her female cousins scolded.

'Shut up,' ordered a male cousin. 'You don't know what you are talking about.'

Students crowded around to see what the commotion was about. I felt like a sardine packed between kids in the hall. Daniel caught my eye and nodded for me to leave quickly. I slipped away to get out of the bullying cousins' sight. I ducked into typing class and took my seat. Looking up, I saw two of the cousins stop at the open doorway. They stood and stared at me for a long, uncomfortable time. Then they disappeared.

A few days later a new Chaldean student came to my theater class. Chaldeans did not usually take theater class, especially the seniors. Though I was a freshman, he wanted to be in my group. The guy was nice and since I had few friends I welcomed his company. I told my family at dinner that there was a new guy in my theater class. 'His name is Nick,' I told them. But Nick turned from nice to mean. He demanded to have the lead role in our group. 'No,' I stated. 'That's my role.'

He pushed me out the back door into a dead-end hallway. 'If you don't let me be the lead,' he said, 'I will make sure your sister gets hurt.'

I thought he was bluffing. 'Go ahead,' I dared. 'Hurt her. But the lead is still mine.'

After that encounter with Nick, I noticed a change in Theresa. No longer the bubbly, life-of-the-party, fun-loving sister, she was solemn and withdrawn. When I saw her like this, Mum would say it was Theresa's PMS time, so initially I chalked it up to hormones. But I soon realized it was more.

The next time theater class met, I told Nick he could have the lead. He took it and failed miserably. The next play we did, Nick wanted the lead again. The teacher said it was someone else's turn and this time I would be the lead actor. Nick had another discussion with me in the dead-end hallway.

'Don't hurt my sister. You can hit me, hurt me, do whatever, but leave Theresa alone,' I pleaded.

He laughed. If the devil had ever come in human form, Nick was it.

On the way home from school one day, Theresa told me to take a different route. You're not my boss, I thought. I left a few minutes after her and held back. I didn't want her to see me. She had been moody and I didn't want to suffer her wrath. Up ahead, I saw a car pull to the side of the street alongside Theresa. I watched her get into the car and the car speed away. Though it was unusual for Theresa to get into someone's car, I assumed it was one of her girlfriends.

That evening, Theresa's mood was extremely foul. She was making dinner for the boys because Mum was at play rehearsal. 'Pat,' Theresa bellowed, 'set the table for dinner.'

'No,' I stated. 'That's your job.'

'You do this right now or I'm going to tell Mum,' she shouted. I turned and walked upstairs. From my bedroom I could hear her slamming dishes and pans.

I was unaware that earlier in the afternoon I had actually seen her being abducted at knifepoint. I didn't think about my sister in the way I should have because I was too caught up in my own problems. Looking back this makes me feel terrible but during that time kids were calling me 'the gay boy'. The night before, Mum was frustrated with me and implied that I was gay. I was tired of the harassment at school and home. I had considered running away for a few months, and this was the night I put my plan into action.

The next morning I left home at the regular time, ditched my schoolbooks and jumped on a city bus only a mile from my house. Before I knew it, I was standing in front of the Greyhound bus station. Two and a half days and a few thousand miles later, I was in Sacramento, California. No one knew where I was until I called Aunt Junie from the bus station. 'You're where?' she asked, incredulous.

'Sacramento,' I said as if I was there for vacation.

That week in California, I learned that my aunt was a lesbian and I had crashed her partner's fortieth birthday bash. And the kids called *me* gay! I was a fourteen-year-old boy at a party with about fifty lesbians. It was surreal.

By the weekend I was back home in Birmingham and unwilling to speak to my mother about what had happened while I was gone. I needed time to process it all. My siblings were more than happy to see me home again. I was surprised they wanted me there. When Theresa was home, she was always locked away in her room, David and Michael just played together and I would stay in my room, reading.

That summer the dark cloud lifted briefly. We traveled on summer vacation and enjoyed being a close-knit family again. But we returned to Birmingham where the dark shadow was waiting for us. That school year, the days were long and sleep was precious. Sleep became the respite from my overwhelming problems. One early morning, I was

awakened by a car parking in the driveway. The doorbell rang. I looked out my window and saw a police
car in the driveway. The doorbell rang again. I heard
my parents get out of bed, go downstairs and open
the front door. Quietly, I stole out of my bedroom and
sat on the top step, out of sight. A police officer was
talking to my parents. His radio squawked loudly and
he turned it down. 'Theresa, where the hell have you
been?' demanded Dad. I could imagine the look of
contempt on Mum's face.

The officer was matter-of-fact. 'Did you even know
your daughter was out tonight?'

'More than likely she was out sluttin' around.' That
was my mum's voice.

The officer questioned my parents about their
slurred speech, suspecting that it was from partying too much the night before and getting to bed late
rather than from still being half asleep.

'We're in our own house,' Mum said defensively.
'You can't do anything about it.'

'Do you realize that your daughter is in extreme
danger?' the officer asked. 'Theresa and I talked on
the way here.'

I heard feet shuffle on the hardwood floor and they
moved into the kitchen. Quietly, I slipped down the
steps to the landing, then two more steps, and craned
my neck to hear what was said.

'I have a good job,' Dad stated. 'We're not leaving just because an officer brings our daughter home late one night.'

I suddenly heard footsteps and leapt up the carpeted steps, jumped into my bed and pulled the blankets over my body. I heard the front door shut and the police car back out of the driveway. I fell asleep to the sound of water. Theresa was in the bath.

By the end of my freshman year of high school we were on the move again. Out of the blue our father was offered a new job on the East Coast, a job that was created just for him. I was excited and thankful to get out of Birmingham. There was never a move I was more relieved to make. After the officer came to our house, I didn't see the Chaldeans as much in the halls and Nick dropped theater class.

Years later, when Theresa and I were both in our mid-twenties and she was pregnant with her first child, I was there to support her. After dropping her husband off at college for his final exam one day, she turned and looked at me. 'Patrick, I have something to tell you.' Her voice wavered. 'Something happened when we lived in Birmingham.'

'You don't have to say anything,' I said. 'I know.'

Dumbfounded, she studied me. 'How do you know?' I recounted the policeman's visit to our house, Nick in my theater class, and the times I was followed by the Chaldeans. We sat in her black Ford Escort and Theresa cried. It was the beginning of her journey. Today, my sister continues on that journey, warning people that human trafficking happens to people of any class and any race. More than a statistic, my big sister is a strong, loving and courageous woman. I'm proud to be her little brother.

A note from Mike

When Theresa told me what had happened to her, not for a second did I think she was fabricating a tale. Why did she choose to tell me? She says she trusted me, and felt comfortable, safe and secure with me. This was the first time she felt that way with someone since those horrific years in Michigan.

Theresa and I were in love. Our story began with a rose. The university had organised a fundraiser in which you could send a rose with a message to someone special. As the resident assistant on check-in day at university, I was busy helping students find the right room. I honestly didn't remember meeting her that first day but then a single rose showed up with my name on it.

I tracked down Theresa, a bubbly lady with a

pretty smile and infectious giggle. We started dating. She was loving and affectionate. However, I started noticing little things that led me to believe there was something she wasn't telling me. I had some formal training in personal observation skills as part of my RA job. I also majored in personnel issues and minored in psychology. I was a fairly good judge of character.

Theresa came from a wealthy family. Her hometown at that time was one of the more affluent communities in our state. I had spent most of my life with my mum, living a low- to middle-class lifestyle. Born in Pittsburgh, I lived a few lean years in Miami before moving to Indiana. I grew up in a mostly white community but frequently traveled to the diverse city of Chicago where there were blacks, Hispanics, Italians and eastern Europeans. I didn't see colors or cultures, only individuals.

Theresa had strong family ties. Her brothers were particularly important to her. She idolized her mother and loved and respected her father. Theresa didn't think she was from a rich family. Once I asked how much money her dad made. Theresa had no idea. And she wasn't about to ask – it just wasn't the thing to do. To me, they were the perfect rich family.

I couldn't understand how revered and feared her dad was. He was a personable guy and we chatted when I visited her home. I knew he was a bigwig in a major American company. But I didn't understand the pecking order of the upper class. Theresa talked about Connecticut, but didn't say much about her time in Michigan.

The campus we were on was picturesque. While we walked hand in hand, once in a while, Theresa would grab my arm tighter. When I looked questioningly at her, she said she felt a chill or that she really loved me. I noticed that she would clutch tightly to me when we passed certain groups of men, usually Middle Eastern men.

One night I playfully snapped my belt, and Theresa cowered in fear. After all the time we had spent together, she was suddenly terrified of me. That's when she told me of her unimaginable life in Michigan. She sat on the floor looking up at me, gauging my reaction to her words. I didn't say a whole lot; what could be said? It's hard to say how long it took for her to tell her story. It didn't matter. All I know is that this girl had experienced unimaginable events.

Her account obviously took me by surprise but I think my reaction took her by surprise. 'I believe you,' I assured her. 'I love you.'

'Still?' she said. 'After you know this about me?'

'I was in love with you before, so what's different now?'

Even so, I had plenty of questions. How could this happen? How could her parents not know? How did she survive?

The events she described lined up with the way she reacted to certain situations. I wasn't sure what to do for her. I encouraged her to let the university police know and I helped her see a therapist. She needed someone else to talk to, to confide in. Her biggest stumbling block was her family. 'I think you should tell them,' I said.

She shook her head. 'I can't.'

In the summer of 1987 we both graduated and drifted apart. For twenty years we didn't have contact with each other, though I frequently wondered how she was dealing with her ordeal and whether she was leading a normal life. One day, while reading my 2007 university alumni magazine, I saw Theresa's name. As an alumnus, there was an entry that she had just written a book. I emailed a mutual friend, and the next day Theresa telephoned. She sounded great and told me about her efforts to help others who have been in her position and, more importantly, how she aimed to prevent these horrific things from happening to others.

Afterword

As a parent myself, I know we strive to protect our children, develop their esteem and encourage them to tell us when something wrong is happening to them. It is equally important to educate the world to identify people who are bullying and preying on children. As adults, as the guardians of our families and our communities, we must step forward and stop it.

My parents didn't know what was happening to me but I am convinced that my teachers, the school security guard and the policeman did know. Yet they did nothing. That is as equally evil and abusive as what my captors did to me. I was good at hiding the facts, covering and keeping the secret. My life depended upon it. For the most part, my parents trusted me. That was born out of their love for me.

They did the best they could at that point in our lives.

I know that some people will not understand why I chose not to tell my parents immediately about the rape. Date rape was not a common term in the early 1980s. Girls weren't educated on this in physical education class like they are now. There were no posters that read, 'Just say no.' I have pondered why I didn't walk in the front door and tell my mother everything.

Firstly, I felt incredible shock at what had just happened. I felt guilty that I had disobeyed my mother's instructions and gone home with a boy. I was not being honest about where I was. My parents believed I was at track practice and had I been where I was supposed to be, none of it would have happened. The thought of revealing to my mother that I had been foolish, acted in direct disobedience to her, and suffered the worst humiliation of my life, was too much. I judged myself guilty. I perceived that it was my fault.

Secondly, there were family dynamics involved. My mother was raised a strict Catholic and ended up pregnant at a young age in the 1960s. Her family pressured her to marry my dad, though they were not happy about it. Begrudgingly, she became a mum and a wife. As I grew older, being her only daughter, she told me many times that I was to remain a virgin until marriage. While sex was a wonderful thing, she said, if I got pregnant, she would throw me out and I was never to return home.

When I was raped, I felt there was no way I could tell them. It would devastate them to know I was no longer a virgin; I had done precisely what Mum had predicted and disobeyed them. It would have crushed them. Like Adam and Eve who hid from God, I was ashamed and hid the truth from my parents. In the back of my mind, I was convinced that if the truth was revealed, I would have had to leave my family.

My parents believed a family should solve their own problems privately. If something terrible happens, it becomes a family secret and is never discussed again. I feel strongly that had I told them about the rape, they would not have called the police or filed charges against the boy. In their eyes, I would have been the guilty party and been punished as such.

My extended family didn't suspect a problem because they all lived in other states and I didn't have longtime friends since we moved so often. So there was no support network, no one to help out when things got tough, no one to confide in and no one to notice changes taking place in my life. These were crucial contributing factors that made me vulnerable. If you recall, Janie had similar vulnerabilities. Traffickers are experts at knowing who to prey upon.

I do not wish for anyone who reads this book to

view my parents as anything except good, providing and loving parents. For many years, it was my decision not to tell them what had happened. After we moved, it took a lot of time to recover and heal from the trauma of those long years. I tried to forget and reconstruct my life. I finally had the life I wanted and was starting over. I got involved in school activities, developed a pleasant group of friends, and met a nice, shy boyfriend who was safely not physical or affectionate with me. I didn't want to mess up my new life, so I shoved the past deep inside. But I was a long way from happy. I suffered from PTSD almost every day.

Still not wanting to disappoint my parents, I went to college and did what I thought was expected of me. After I graduated, I told my parents an abbreviated version of the abuse and slavery. Even as an adult, I couldn't bring myself to tell them everything. I was their little girl. I still wanted their approval. Though it no longer mattered that I wasn't a virgin, I didn't want to hurt them.

I did want to correct their misconception that I had been out 'having fun with the Arabs'. I tried to convince them that I wasn't acting on my own choices back then. To this day, they don't know the entire story in its horrific detail. It is difficult for us to discuss. What parent wants to believe they didn't protect their child? In my heart, I know that if they had known what was happening, they would have moved heaven and earth to save me.

When I began doing interviews and speaking out publicly, I struggled with whether to reveal my identity. Should I change my name? Should I be anonymous and hide my face? Would this affect my career, my children's lives, my family's reputation or my safety? There were pros and cons to both sides. In the end I decided that if I was going to do this, I should do it one hundred per cent. Continuing to hide only allowed those men to control my life and my freedom all these years later. I realize that at any moment they could find out that I have written this book and told my story to the world. But decades later, I am nothing to them. Perhaps their male children are now doing the same, and worse, to young girls.

Was I afraid? Yes. But I'm more afraid that this will continue to occur in America, as well as other countries, if no one dares to speak out, if no one puts a face to the victims and if no one gives victims a voice. If this can happen in America, the land of the free, it can happen anywhere. I would be as guilty as those who did nothing to help me if I let my story grow cold on the pages. Together, we can stop modern slavery. Together, we can stand against those who bully, intimidate and violate others. Secrets lose their power when they are no longer secrets. My decision is to share this so that other people will know that human trafficking takes on many forms, happens anywhere, and can happen to any kid. The most important message of this book is that sexual slavery can happen to anyone.

I regularly get calls that a teenager has been found and needs help. As word gets out and people become educated and recognize the signs, we see how prevalent this crime is. We are seeing more and more headlines reporting these incidents.

I meet with emergency and medical personnel across the nation to educate them on what to look for and how to help. These girls live a violent life. Frequently they are first seen by emergency and medical personnel. But because these caring professions don't know what they are dealing with, they patch up the girls and send them right back into it.

In the beginning when I started speaking out and sharing my story, I noticed I would get a few women come up to me after and shake my hand or ask if they could hug me, give me a look in my eyes and say, 'Thank you'. I just knew they had endured something similar. But I still felt like I was the only one that something like this had happened to.

Now as there is more awareness about this issue, it is not uncommon for at least two women to whisper in my ear, 'My story is just like yours!' and then walk away.

Not a day goes by that I ever regret the decision to publish my story, to speak publicly, or show my face on television to tell what happened to a normal kid from the suburbs. This is my purpose. It is not easy. I battle with feelings of being unworthy, and a bad book review by a stranger who isn't educated on the topic of human trafficking can be devastating. When I speak at a conference and a counselor tells me that she is working with a child who is being sexually exploited commercially, and that my story opened her eyes, then it is worth the pain.

My teenage daughter was ridiculed by some unkind acquaintances who insinuated that I am unhealthy and unclean. My daughter took it in her stride, defended me, and grew stronger for it. There will always be cruel and unsupportive people who do not understand. There will be family members of the opinion that I should stay quiet, protect the family name and brush my bad experience under the rug.

After my escape, I decided to dedicate my life to helping others. I graduated college and became a licensed social worker. I attended graduate school where I trained as a guidance counselor. I remained a social worker, working with pregnant and parenting teens. Blessed that I escaped my horrible trial, I want to make life easier for others.

Several years after college, I married and began a family. I made a decision that I would never let those evil men continue to own me. Though I shut away the horrible memories, they surfaced at night in my nightmares. Unfortunately, there was a great deal more damage than I realized or cared to admit. My marriage did not survive. Relationships were difficult for me. I desperately wanted a savior, a protector. Yet I never found anyone who could provide what I needed, or who accepted my dark past and emotional scars.

It has been a long journey of healing. I'm better at taking down the facade of always being strong while fighting the demons inside myself. Now that the sinister secret is out in the open, I plan to live the rest of my life raising my three beautiful children, keeping them safe from harm, and helping them have high self-esteem.

I want to educate society on the horrors of trafficking, and give hope and healing to those who have suffered unbearable things. For those who have been abused, I carry the message that life can get better. My goal is to help others and be a catalyst to end sexual slavery.

Slavery still exists. It needs to stop. Now.

I was in the rare five per cent of trafficking victims who don't experience incestuous relations. I hadn't been physically abused at home and my parents weren't drug addicts. I was in the rare two per cent who came from a family that was still intact while I was victimized.

While the majority of children at risk are youths from broken and abusive homes, the foster family system, or runaways, this doesn't mean that any other child who does not come from such a social group is not at risk. There are children who live in secure, middle-class homes who have parents who are unaware of their children's involvement in pornography and prostitution. Insidious and undetectable, many law enforcement officers and child welfare agencies do not realize the scope of the problem. Dr Estes calls child sexual exploitation the most hidden form of child abuse in the US and North America.

There is no stereotypical look for traffickers and pimps. They come from all walks of life and socio-economic backgrounds. Both men and women from all races and religions, from esteemed doctors and wealthy business owners, to plantation owners and farmers. From hoodlums from the ghetto to women that were similarly victimized themselves. They come in all forms.

Because traffickers aim to have complete control over someone's identity, it can potentially happen any-where, to anyone. In reality, I belonged to Jonathan, though it seemed as if I belonged to Nick. But Nick was just the middleman. As with victims, traffickers cannot be identified by specific socio-economic or racial characteristics, though it is more common among cultures that don't value women. Traffickers range from familial, mum-and-pop operations, to highly organized networks that are international business. Generally, they are organized and connected with contacts in many cities.

Experts at beating down their victims with emotional and mental abuse until they are too scared to tell anyone, their tools include force, torture, manipulation, and coercion. Psychologically and physically, the message is the same. The victim is valueless. Worthless. Sexual slavery is about controlling people.

In his book, *New Slavery*, Kevin Bales states that it also involves an economic relationship. Though I did not realize this at the time, it certainly related to my situation. I was used as a reward and incentive for others to perform better or produce more. I was a prize for a job well done. While I was living it, I never considered the economic nature of my slavery. I didn't collect money after sex acts, and I didn't see Nick receive money from the men. It is possible that this may have taken place in the other room where the men gathered, waiting their turn.

As I entered these men-only dens, while my eyes adjusted to the smoke and darkness, I could see the coffee tables piled with drinks, cigarettes, and lots and lots of cash. It is clear to me now that it was a business transaction that had been arranged prior to my arrival, and that I was a component of that deal. The conditions were understood by everyone except me. My role was also a business transaction between Nick, and Jonathan, and myself. I was working off the price of the pictures. As long as I was profitable to them, they worked to control me to ensure that this arrangement continued.

In addition to coercion and an economic factor, another core characteristic of slavery is violence. Bales mentions that slavery is about having no control, no choices and feeling an ever-present fear of violence. Many victims are tricked into trafficking. Once in, the person is usually enslaved until death. Murder and suicide are the most common means of escape for most victims. The key to the trafficker is that the girl loses their free will. I certainly felt that I had no choice but to submit, to do as I was told or be severely punished. My loved ones would have been harmed or killed if I hadn't and that was not an option to me.

It is extremely challenging for people to comprehend this topic. Most would like to turn away from it, deny it happens or re-victimize the survivor by not believing them, requiring them to prove their story, or stating they must have had a choice. Everyone in

America has free will, right? This is the land of the free, right? Everyone has options and choices, right?

Unfortunately, that is not the case. Anti-human trafficking advocates bring awareness to the public about trafficking, re-educate people regarding slavery, and attempt to re-frame people's beliefs regarding prostitution. It is such a daunting task that keeps us busy trying to change the mentality of people, and fighting for the voiceless to be understood, that we often have little time or energy left to save the victim. But one cannot be done without the other.

Lisa Thompson of the Salvation Army states it perfectly in a recent email posted on Dignity List-Serv: '... one article details how a young girl was violently forced into the sex trade and how she ultimately accepted her role as prostitute and tried to attract buyers. Professionals in the field of torture, domestic violence child sexual abuse, and commercial sexual exploitation refer to this process as seasoning, grooming, or conditioning. In 1973, Amnesty International described the coercive techniques (besides physical torture) used to gain control of political prisoners; techniques such as isolation, induced debility, exhaustion, threats, degradation, enforcing of trivial demands, and the granting of occasional indulgences, to mention a few. These are the same means (as well as physical torture) that are used to subjugate women and girls in prostitution and pornography.'

The women and girls we see on the street corner may give every appearance of freely choosing to be there, but the unseen forces that condition them to be there are every bit as real as if they were made of yards of barbed wire. Moreover, if a girl in Cambodia can be conditioned into prostitution, why can't an American woman or girl? Given the conditioning that occurs, how then can any casual observer judge whether someone is a forced prostitute or a voluntary one? If someone who was forced into prostitution becomes conditioned to the life, and accepts their fate, are they now a voluntary prostitute? If a twelve-year-old is given money or a meal to eat in exchange for sex, is she now a prostitute?

What child grows up with dreams of being a prostitute? In school when they're asked 'What do you want to be when you grow up?', what student says 'prostitute' or 'stripper' is their desired ambition? Not one. And how many children do this voluntarily? Not one. They don't take home 100 per cent of the revenue they made at the end of the night, they give it all to someone.

The cold, hard facts are that prostitution is, in most cases, a form of human trafficking, except in the very rare instances when a woman has autonomy over the work she chooses to do and keeps the money for herself. But notice that I used the word 'woman' – there is no such thing as consent in teen or child prostitution. And if a woman has a pimp, then she is being trafficked. Even if she believes he loves her and is her boyfriend.

Human trafficking has many faces but if we all club together I hope we can begin to stamp them out.

Resources

If you've been moved by Theresa's story and want to get involved in helping make slavery history, there are organizations that are working tirelessly to end human trafficking of every kind in every country.

You can learn more about Theresa's organization Traffickfree at www.traffickfree.com, and about how you can help educate and bring awareness to others in your community so innocent people do not fall into the same hopeless cycle.

Here are some other recommended organizations:

Not for Sale
www.NotForSaleCampaign.org

Doma International
www.domaconnection.org

Love146
www.love146.org

Be Free Dayton
www.befreedayton.org

Stop Child Trafficking Now
www.sctnow.org

VCOM: Women & Children in Crisis
www.vineyardcollege.org

Polaris Project
www.PolarisProject.org

Free the Slaves
www.FreeTheSlaves.net

International Justice Mission
www.IJM.org

Shared Hope International
www.SharedHope.org

Unseen UK
www.UnseenUK.org

Salvation Army
www.salvationarmy.org

Soroptimist International
www.soroptimistinternational.org